The Conquest of the North and South Poles

ADVENTURES OF THE PEARY AND BYRD EXPEDITIONS

★

BY RUSSELL OWEN

ILLUSTRATED BY LYND WARD

RANDOM HOUSE · NEW YORK

ACKNOWLEDGMENTS

The author expresses his thanks to the holders of the copyrights
for the use of certain material taken from the following sources:
From *The Log of Bob Bartlett*, by Captain Robert A. Bartlett.
Copyright 1928 by G. P. Putnam's Sons. Courtesy of G. P. Put-
nam's Sons. From *A Tenderfoot with Peary*, by George Borup.
Copyright 1911, 1939 by Mrs. Yvette B. Andrews. Reprinted by
permission of the publishers, J. B. Lippincott Company. From *The
North Pole*, by Admiral Robert E. Peary. Copyright 1910, 1938 by
Robert E. Peary. Reprinted by permission of the publishers,
J. B. Lippincott Company. From *The Snowbaby's Own Story*, by
Marie Ahnighito Peary. Copyright 1934 by J. B. Lippincott Co.
Reprinted by permission of the publishers, J. B. Lippincott Com-
pany. From *Peary, The Man Who Refused to Fail*, by Fitzhugh
Green. Reprinted by permission of G. P. Putnam's Sons. From
How Peary Reached the Pole, by Donald Macmillan. Reprinted by
permission of Houghton Mifflin Company. From *Nearest the Pole*,
by Robert E. Peary. Reprinted by permission of Doubleday & Co.

"The true explorer does his work not for any hope of rewards or honor, but because the thing he has set himself to do is a part of his very being, and must be accomplished for the sake of accomplishment, and he counts lightly hardships, risks, obstacles, if only they do not bar him from his goal."

Robert E. Peary

CONTENTS

part one
THE NORTH POLE

part two
THE SOUTH POLE

ROBERT E. PEARY and Richard E. Byrd have been our most popular polar explorers.

They were both in the United States Navy, although neither of them had much to do with ships. Peary was an engineer and Byrd was an airplane pilot.

Peary was the first man to reach the North Pole, after years of trying to get there. He went on foot, with dogs and sledges.

Byrd was the first to fly to the North Pole and the South Pole.

And both men were made Rear Admiral in recognition of what they had done.

During the years in which Peary worked in the north, and learned how to live there, he became the greatest polar traveler of his time.

American prestige in the north was low when Peary started his explorations, and he brought back to this country a feeling of pride, and success in the polar regions.

It made him one of our heroes.

When Byrd started exploration by air nobody had been able to reach the North Pole or the South Pole by air. Roald Amundsen, who first reached the South Pole on foot, had tried to go to the North Pole by air, but had failed.

Up to Byrd's time explorers in the polar regions had been forced to toil over the surface. He proved that an airplane can be used to find new land, that in a few hours one can go over distances that would take weeks or months to cross on foot.

And by photographs taken continually when he was flying, he was able to bring back a record of the kind of land over which he flew. It was a new way of mapping.

When he began his polar work engines were not very powerful, and airplanes were not always reliable. But he showed how they could be put to work; today air travel is used in most of our polar exploration.

The methods that Byrd developed as a pioneer have now become the simple ways of doing things in the polar regions. Men fly over the North Pole every few days, testing navigation, hunting for new currents and movements of the ice, making weather observations, discovering many queer things.

Human beings will always want to know about the unknown, and there is still a great deal to be done by those who have the desire to explore. Most of the north polar regions have been mapped now, but much of the Antarctic, the south polar region, is still unknown. It is a big place.

Explorers still use the tool of Byrd—the airplane —for seeing a great continent. And they use the ways of Peary—on foot—for geological and close inspection. They are new and improved ways, but basically the two methods are the same.

It is for these things that Peary and Byrd will be remembered.

RUSSELL OWEN

PART ONE

The North Pole

I

FOR hundreds of years men had been trying to get to the North Pole.

The first people to come in contact with the polar ice were probably the Vikings. They discovered Iceland and Greenland, and reached America long before Columbus. It was the Vikings who learned that the cold of the Arctic did not kill.

For some reason there came into being an idea that there was open water north of the polar ice. This led to later efforts of discoverers.

After America was found by Columbus in 1492,

men tried in many ways to get around the New
World that barred their way to China. China was
thought to be a land of great wealth, of silks and
spices. Few of the early voyagers wanted anything
to do with the new land, which they thought was
only full of Indians.

So they pushed north, at first to find a way to the
open polar sea.

As far back as 1607 Henry Hudson, who was one
of the first great explorers by sea, tried to get to the
pole by way of the east coast of Greenland. Hudson
then tried to go north near Spitzbergen, but was
stopped by ice.

Later, he sailed up the Hudson River, hoping it
would give him a passage to China. In addition to
the river, other bodies of water which bear his name
are: the Hudson Straits between Labrador and Baf-
fin Land, and Hudson Bay, where he died after being cast adrift in a small boat by his men.

Long after, in 1827, Edward Parry also tried to
go north from Spitzbergen. He left his ship and went
on over the ice, his party pulling boats on sledges
behind them. The English never trusted to the pulling power of dogs on the ice. Even when they had
dogs, they did not know how to use them.

An English expedition in the little ship *Alert*
made its way to Grant Land in 1875, and Albert
Markham reached 83 degrees, 20 minutes. (The

pole is 90 degrees. And a degree is 60 geographical miles.)

An American expedition in the *Jeanette* tried to drift across the pole from Bering Strait, but the ship was crushed in the ice. Only a few men survived.

Then the tragic Greely expedition went up to Fort Conger in Grant Land in 1881. Most of the men died of starvation, but a man named Lockwood got as far north as 83 degrees, 24 minutes, on the west Greenland coast.

And finally in 1893, Fridtjof Nansen, a famous Norwegian explorer, put out from the Siberian shore in the hope of drifting across the pole. The ship did not go near the pole, but Nansen and a companion tried to reach it by sledge, after leaving the ship.

They failed, and after a long struggle over the ice finally reached Franz Josef Land. The ship later came out of the ice near Spitzbergen.

By this time, of course, the idea of an open polar sea had been given up. But men still hoped that Greenland went far north near the pole.

In the north many men had died; others had disappeared. But the lure of the pole still called.

2

ALL of Robert E. Peary's early life helped to prepare him for exploration in the north. In person, too, he appeared to be a man destined for great and difficult tasks. He was tall, with wide shoulders and a deep chest. A flowing mustache hung down on each side of his mouth, and, during later years, his face became lined and marked from facing into bitter winds.

His ancestors had been hardy folk who lived in Maine. Robert Edwin Peary was born on May 6, 1856, in Cambria County, Pennsylvania, where his parents had moved not long before. After his father died his mother moved back to her people in Maine, and Peary grew up in what is now part of Portland.

After leaving high school he went to Bowdoin College, where he was a good athlete and an equally good student of civil engineering. Indeed, one of his professors said that he learned as much from Peary as Peary did from him.

In those days, men used their legs, and Peary thought nothing of taking a walk of twenty-five miles. Once he walked thirty miles in eight hours and a half. He rowed on the college crew, and once threw a baseball 316 feet, beating all his competitors. In addition, he was a good swimmer and sailor.

After he was graduated from Bowdoin he became town surveyor in Fryeburg, Maine. However, he didn't lose his taste for a number of skills and sports. He liked to slide downhill in the winter time, he took part in skating parties, and even in theatricals. He tried to learn to sing. Breaking raw colts to riding horses was one of his diversions. He learned to draw, too, an ability which was handy for sketching when in later years he went north. In fact, there was almost nothing that Peary would not try to do and do well.

Knowing this, it is not surprising that, although he made his reputation in the Arctic Zone, he began his explorations in the tropics.

He had gone to Washington as a draftsman in the Coast and Geodetic Survey for ten dollars a week. That doesn't seem much nowadays, but to Peary it was a start.

While there he took an examination for membership in the Civil Engineer Corps of the United States Navy. Two hundred men took the test; only four men passed—and of these Peary was one. Soon after he was on his way to Nicaragua in Central America.

Because of its lakes and rivers, Nicaragua has always seemed to be an ideal spot for a canal between the Atlantic and the Pacific. At that time no canal had yet been built, although a Frenchman named de Lesseps had tried to construct one at Panama. It was Peary's belief that some day there would be two canals: one at Panama and the other across Nicaragua.

Peary was twenty-eight years old when he went south with the Nicaraguan expedition in 1884. He plunged into an almost impassable jungle, on one of the most difficult survey jobs a man could attempt. He had to climb trees to find how he could best travel forward; he forced his way with others through streams and mud, sleeping at night in the open.

It was during this expedition that Peary first mentioned in his diary the attraction of polar exploration. When he returned home, he found in an old pamphlet a description of the inland ice of Greenland, which again stirred his imagination.

Little was known then of northern Greenland, or how far north the land went. We know now that it is the largest and most northern island in the world. This island, thirteen times the size of Pennsylvania, is nothing but a huge bowl of snow and ice 9,000 feet high, hemmed in by mountains along the rim.

Peary thought Greenland might reach as far north as the pole. Possibly by traveling north over the island, he could reach the pole and walk across it.

The sun shines in Greenland for a few months, and near the coast the summers are warm. But as soon as the sun goes below the horizon—where it remains for a good part of the year—Greenland becomes a land of freezing cold and howling blizzards.

To young Peary, just returned from the tropics, the call of the north was strong. No one had ever attempted to cross to the east coast of Greenland, so he determined to go north and then work his way inland as far as possible. In this way, he would learn something of polar travel. It was to be largely an experimental trip.

In 1886 he went north for the first time, and started inland from a fjord east of Disco Island. His only companion was Christian Maigaard. The two

men crossed many crevasses, and fell into some, but luckily got out of them.

They crossed lakes and rivers in the snow and ice. Peary slipped into one of the rivers that ran between walls of ice, was swept away in its waters, and narrowly escaped drowning. The explorers went inland a hundred miles before they had to turn back.

When Peary returned to Washington the Nicaraguan canal again demanded his time, and in 1887 he went back there in charge of another survey. This task lasted almost a year, but it was his last work in the tropics.

Peary now took a partner who helped him greatly in his later work. He had fallen in love with Josephine Diebitsch, daughter of a professor in the Smithsonian Institution. Peary and Miss Diebitsch were married in Washington in August, 1888.

During this time, the North Pole had lost none of its attractiveness for Peary. He now mapped out a daring bit of exploration. Nansen had crossed the lower part of Greenland, but the interior was still a blank space on the maps. This was also true of much of the north and northeast coasts. Peary was determined to explore these regions.

He obtained leave from the Navy and started north again on June 6, 1891. In his party were his wife and a number of scientists.

The expedition's physician was Dr. Frederick A. Cook, who was later to claim that he reached the pole just before Peary made his successful trip. Few people today believe that Cook ever got there, although he was an experienced ice traveler. However, after Peary's return from the pole, Cook's claims caused an uproar.

On this trip Peary made his winter base at Inglefield Gulf, far up the northwest coast of Greenland. He planned a journey to the northeast that would cover 1,200 miles. Small parties, he had decided, were much more efficient than large ones for fast and safe travel, and he took with him only one person, Eivind Astrup.

They had three sledges, twenty dogs, food, and instruments. Peary and his companion slept on the snow in their furs like the Eskimos, although the temperature was often far below zero. When they were overtaken by storms they crept into drifts to sleep.

Traveling on, they reached an elevation of 5,700 feet. Then the surface began to slope down again to the eastern side. On June 26 they saw patches of land where the snow had disappeared.

On July 1 they started down into a wide valley in the ice, and the air became so much warmer that it was uncomfortable.

They found some musk oxen in the valley, and shot several as food for themselves and the dogs. Finally they climbed up 3,800 feet to a rocky plateau.

Before them to the east was a great arm of the sea which Peary called Independence Bay because it was first seen on the Fourth of July. And to the north stretched land and mountains and glaciers that no man had even seen before.

The land is now called Peary Land.

There was, so Peary wrote, "brilliant sunshine

all about us, with yellow poppies growing between the rocks around our feet, and a herd of musk oxen in the valley behind us. Down in that same valley I had found an old friend, a dandelion in bloom, and had seen the bullet-like flight and heard the energetic buzz of the bumble-bee."

Yet this place, with a temperature of seventy degrees on the day of its discovery, was only a little more than 500 miles from the North Pole. Greenland, the whole north land, in fact, has many flowers and insects in the summer time, when the sun always shines.

With his food supply low, Peary went as far southeast as he dared, and then turned back across the cold interior to his camp. At one time, when he had reached an elevation of over 7,000 feet, he was held up by a storm for sixty hours.

He returned safely to camp, having completed what was possibly the greatest sledge journey made up to that time. He had traveled more than 1,200 miles over the icy interior, had found new lands, and returned without any serious mishap.

His success laid the basis for his reputation and his later work. Explorers called it a feat second only to that of reaching the pole.

His great adventure was to be followed by crushing defeats for many years. But he was just getting started.

FAILURE

3

_____

PEARY had had amazing luck in his first probings into the Arctic.

It encouraged him so much that he attempted to do even more on his next trip.

His second Greenland expedition left Philadelphia in June, 1893. Mrs. Peary went with him again, and as she was expecting a baby she took a nurse, Mrs. Susan J. Cross. The baby—the first white child to be born so far north—arrived in Greenland on September 12. She was named Marie Ahnighito Peary.

Then, in the spring of 1894, Peary made his first

15

great mistake—he tried to use too many men. The unusually bitter weather on the ice cap and the punishing effect it had on the dogs defeated him.

His party of eight men gradually succumbed to illness and frost. Compelled at last to turn back, he brought to an end one of his most humiliating and unsuccessful trips. The brash young man who had plunged into the Arctic had not made good.

When his wife returned to the United States in 1895, Peary was left with only Matt Henson and Hugh J. Lee. The courageous Henson, who was colored, had been Peary's servant in Nicaragua, and was turning into a remarkably good dog driver and Arctic traveler.

On April 1, 1895, Peary, Henson and Lee again started for Independence Bay. They hauled themselves and their baggage up over the ledge, past crevasses, and into the interior where they reached a point 6,500 feet above sea level. Here they had trouble with the dogs and Lee became ill. These major problems, together with some others that developed later, made their situation serious.

Eventually they could see the land ahead, but when they reached lower ground they were unable to find game.

Nevertheless, they decided to push on.

"I felt then, as I feel now," wrote Peary, "that in that cool deliberate moment we took the golden bowl of life in our hands, and that the bowl had suddenly become very fragile."

All the poet in Peary, all his natural daring, all that he had made of himself as a young man, came out in that statement.

But he was discouraged. He had gone as far as he had before, but no farther.

When they reached the land near Independence Bay they found plenty of musk oxen, and ate their fill of raw meat. This they shared with the few dogs that remained after illness had cut their numbers.

After the weather had cleared Peary had a good view of a great mountain and of land to the north.

He was also able to outline more of the coast of Independence Bay. But he had shot his bolt on this expedition that lasted two years.

That he and his companions returned at all was a wonder. The sledge was smashed and had to be

rebuilt before they could attempt the 600-mile trip back to their home base. When the sledge was ready, it seemed that the worst was over; but they had gone only part of the way when Lee became so ill that he could not walk. He dropped on the snow and told Peary and Henson to go on without him.

Peary said: "We will all get home or none of us will."

We have it on the sick man's word that for a whole day Peary nursed him like a baby. He fed him carefully from his small medical stock, and the next day Lee was better and could go on.

They averaged a little more than twenty miles a day and, worn out, but pushing on with incredible fortitude, managed to get to the west coast over the crevasses and rocks.

During the last of their march Peary crossed the delicate snow bridges over the crevasses as though he were half awake. It seemed to Lee and Henson that their leader almost hoped to fall into one of the deep openings in the ice.

So strong was this impression that Lee removed the cartridges from the rifles, so that Peary would not be able to use one of them on himself.

4

ALTHOUGH Peary's second trip across Greenland failed to add much to his former exploration, he still stood forth in the minds of many men here and abroad as the best ice traveler of his time.

He had found new land. He had shown that the two coasts of Greenland came together toward the north. This led him to believe that Greenland was an island. It was also fairly obvious that the most northerly body of land was either Greenland or the top of Grant Land to the west.

Furthermore, some remarkable meteorites, which may be seen today at the American Museum of Natural History in New York, had been brought back.

After his failure of 1895 Peary gave up his idea of trying to reach the pole over the Greenland ice cap.

He decided to take a ship as far north as he could through the famous Kennedy and Robeson Channels which make up the passageway between Grinnell Land and Greenland. Although the channels were often choked with drifting ice that came down from the polar sea, Peary thought he could force his way through them as he traveled north. If his efforts were successful he could make a base on Grinnell Land or Grant Land to the west of Greenland.

In his search for a stout ship to make this difficult journey, he was aided by the British, who had been pioneers in the efforts to find a way to the pole and the Northwest Passage. Discouraged at last by repeated failures, they had given up the attempt and turned their attention to the Antarctic. It seemed that they had done all that it was possible for men to do.

The *Windward,* a British vessel that had been used in polar work, was now offered to Peary by Alfred Harmsworth, later Lord Northcliffe. Harmsworth even offered to have the *Windward*'s decrepit engines repaired or replaced, but this was not done for lack of time.

Peary decided to go north again in 1898. At that time our country was at war with Spain, but the explorer was given five years' leave from the Navy. Proceeding north, he conducted his own war against the numbing cold. When he reached Kane Basin, the ice was too thick to permit passage, and he was forced to winter at Cape D'Urville, the southernmost part of Grinnell Land.

It must be remembered that the island just west of Greenland is really split into three parts by deep fjords, or inlets. The whole island has been given the name Ellsmere Island. But the southernmost part is called Ellsmere Land, the central part Grinnell Land, and the northern part, which Peary was to make famous, is Grant Land.

His only chance to get toward the pole was to take supplies and food farther north by sled from Cape D'Urville, and then make his attack on the polar sea. No explorer had ever tried to travel in winter time, but Peary was sure it could be done.

It was now December. The sun had gone down to stay below the horizon for months, and there was little moon, for this was the middle of the winter night. The temperature was more than fifty degrees below zero with a bitter wind.

Peary wanted to reach Fort Conger, up in Grant Land. There was a hut there that had been used by another explorer, who had also left some food. Although Fort Conger was 250 miles from the ship, Peary hoped to reach it in five days, for he was a fast traveler.

But the ice had been heaped up badly by pressure. As you know, water expands, taking up more space when it freezes. The ice in the channel was in a limited space. It could not expand outward, so as it froze, it broke and became heaped up. Sometimes chunks of it were forced nearly a hundred feet up the rocky cliffs from the frozen channel.

Although Peary's sledges were light, he and his Eskimos scrambled and grunted and lifted over the rough surface. Sledges broke, and dogs were exhausted. So were the men.

Finally, through darkness and cold, Peary stumbled through the last heap of broken ice and into the abandoned hut at Fort Conger. He hoped to find something to eat, but the food had been left carelessly and most of it was spoiled.

Bad as this disappointment was, there was something worse in store. Peary discovered that his feet were frozen. In the darkness there was nothing he could do except lie on a bunk in his furs, while the Eskimos groped their way around and tried to find something to eat.

As Peary's feet thawed out they hurt badly, and he realized that he would lose most of his toes. The pain was so great that he could not stand.

Nevertheless, he made plans for going ahead while he lay there. Later Bob Bartlett, his captain and one of his sledging companions, said to Peary:

"But your feet were frozen, Commander. Didn't it occur to you that the loss of the big toes cripples a man for life?"

"I did worry about that for a time, Bob," Peary answered. "It seemed such a small trouble beside some of the others that I forgot it except when my wretched feet wouldn't let me forget it."

And this from a man who lay on his back in the dark for six long weeks, unable to move! While he lay there he wrote on the wall of the hut:

"I will find a way or make one."

Then the Eskimos strapped him to a sled and hauled him 250 miles over that awful broken ice to his ship. There his frozen toes were removed, all but the little ones.

5

PEARY did not let his crippled feet stop his work. On April 19, 1899, only two months after he left Fort Conger strapped to a sledge, he was on his way back there with supplies.

He had to ride, for he could not stand. But on his journey over rough ice, in twilight, and lashed to his sledge, he averaged twenty-five miles a day. That wasn't bad for a man who could not walk!

When he returned to the ship he became curious about the country to the west. Nothing was known of that part of Grinnell Land. So he had himself tucked up on his sledge, and with Eskimos driving, worked his way up to the ice cap, 4,700 feet high.

He outlined several fjords, which are narrow bays with high cliffs, and far to the west he discovered new land which is now called Axel Heiberg Land. (It was partly explored by Otto Sverdrup, a Norwegian, and named for Axel Heiberg, a wealthy Norwegian who backed him and later helped Amundsen on his trip to the South Pole. Amundsen named a glacier for him in Antarctica.)

It was summer now, but it was still bitterly cold. The ice was rotten and broken, and on it were deep pools of water through which Peary could not ride on a sledge.

He had to get off and walk. Although his feet were not yet healed and pained him at every step, he waded through the ice water that sometimes reached to his chin.

"One can get used to anything," he said, as he limped along.

No doubt, however, the loyalty of the natives made Peary's difficulties less burdensome. They would refuse him nothing, for he treated them well. He gave them guns and ammunition to aid them in their hunt for food. He gave their wives needles and thread.

More important, he was always fair and just. He kept his word, and he expected the Eskimos to keep theirs. The result was that they would go anywhere with him, even when they were afraid of the bad spirits in which they believed.

"Peary was never tired," they said later.

"Peary did not fear the wind or the thin ice, or the spirits of darkness as we did."

Through the next winter he sledged tons of supplies to Fort Conger, whence he intended to take off for the North Pole. Sometimes he made sixty or seventy miles a day, a seemingly impossible feat to those who do not know how rapidly dogs can travel on a smooth surface.

Speaking of this time, Peary said: "The process of breaking in the tendons and muscles of my feet had been disagreeable, but was, I believed, final and complete."

He also made the surprising statement: "I felt that I had no reason to complain."

Early in 1900 he started north again, this time from Fort Conger. He did not know whether he would try to get to the North Pole from Greenland, or from farther west on Grant Land. He finally decided to try by way of Greenland.

Even if he could not push out on the Polar Sea, he could do a good deal of exploring around the north of Greenland, for nobody had ever gone there.

In his party this time there were seven sledges, one of them driven by Matt Henson, who was invaluable to Peary. On many occasions he was sent ahead to find a trail through the broken ice.

They went along just off the Greenland shore, over the sea ice beneath the cliffs and beyond the bays. It was hard going, and often they were held up by blinding snow storms. When that happened they made a house out of snow blocks and waited for the weather to clear a little.

Often they had to make a road, and sometimes ran into ice that had been forced up into ridges nearly fifty feet high. An explorer as experienced in traveling over ice as was Peary knows that open water reflects a black, or dark gray smudge, on the clouds overhead. One day he and his men saw this sign of open water ahead, but when they reached the spot, a thin covering of ice had formed.

They made their way forward on foot carefully and got across safely, but they could not take their sledges. On the way back they brushed the snow off the new ice. This was to permit the cold air to get to it, so that the ice would freeze thicker. The ice did get thicker, and the next day they took the sledges over, keeping them far apart.

Again they ran into rough ice and had to make a road through it. Most of the Eskimos and some of

their dogs had weakened, so Peary went on with only Henson and one Eskimo.

The ice became broken up, and the dogs and sledges fell into the water. Then the party ran into such deep snow that they had to stamp a road through it with snowshoes. They were forced to push the sledges while the dogs pulled to make a little headway. With broken ice, glaciers, huge ridges of smashed cakes, the going was very bad for a good part of the way around northern Greenland.

But Peary went much farther than any man had gone before. He reached the most northerly tip of Greenland, beyond which there was no more land. If he were going to try for the pole there was only one way to do so, and that was to push out on the ice-covered sea.

Far ahead he could detect the dark reflection of water on the sky—water-sky, as it is called—and Peary was not too hopeful.

He went north for three days—only one of them in good weather—over ice ridges that were from twenty-five to fifty feet high. Beyond he could see only broken pack ice on the sea. It was useless to try to go farther.

So he returned and again traveled east along the coast. Sometimes the mountains of ice he passed, smashed up against the stone cliffs, were more than a hundred feet in height. But he went as far as he could down the east coast of a land that has been named after him—Peary Land. Then he realized that he would have to try another route to get to the pole.

He had finished one of the greatest sledging trips ever made when he got back to Fort Conger. And in outlining northern Greenland he had mapped the most northern land on earth.

What an accomplishment for a man with no toes on his feet—a man who was always suffering pain!

Years later, the cairns of stone that he had built to hold his records were found by other explorers.

6

PEARY had been going north for four years, and his leave of absence from the Navy had not expired. Yet he had been urged to return home because of his frozen feet.

"No," he had replied. "When my furlough has expired, or I have reached the pole, I shall be ready to go."

When he returned from Greenland to Fort Conger he found that the Eskimos had killed many musk oxen and seals, but he needed more to feed the men and dogs.

Peary and Henson and some Eskimos went far

inland to get supplies, and as they did not want to haul so much meat back to the camp they made snow igloos and lived in them all winter.

These igloos are a wonderful example of how to make the country work for you. In the north the snow packs down under the cold and heavy winds, and it can be cut out in solid blocks. With these the Eskimos make their igloos very easily, raising one layer of blocks on another, until the dome-shaped top is formed.

Then they dig down at one point so that they can get in and out under the wall of the igloo, without letting the warmer air inside escape. A bench of snow is raised on one side as a sleeping platform. The door is closed tightly with a block of snow.

The igloos will stand heavy storms and can be left on the trail for shelters.

During the period he spent in the igloos Peary saw, as he had in other winters, the beauty of the aurora borealis. This takes the form of streaks of many-colored lights that wave and pulsate across the skies of the north. Sometimes they appear in the northern part of the United States, where they are known as northern lights. Here they take on the form of beams, like searchlight beams, weaving back and forth over the sky. They do not seem quite as strong in the Arctic as in the Antarctic, although they are always beautiful.

That year Peary could not make an attempt to reach the North Pole, as neither men nor dogs were in good enough condition. But he did go north for a time and then went south to Ellsmere Land to see if a ship had arrived from the States.

On the way he met some Eskimos, and the talk that followed is typical of Eskimos. They never offer any information; it has to be pried out of them.

"Did the ship get up last year?" asked Peary.

"Yes," an Eskimo replied.

"Who was the captain?"

"Captain Sam."

Peary pressed on: "Who was the steward?"

"Old Charlie."

"Anyone else on board that I knew?" asked Peary.

"Mitty Peary and Ahnighito."

"When did the ship go back?"

"Oh," said one of the Eskimos. "Didn't go back. Right in Payer Harbor."

So, much to Peary's amazement, he learned that his wife, "Mitty Perry," and his daughter, Ahnighito, were waiting for him! From the replies given him, he also knew that their ship had been frozen in long before, so that they could not return.

He set out for the ship so rapidly that he left the startled Eskimos far behind. They couldn't imagine anyone being so anxious to see his family again!

Husband, wife, and daughter came together in a joyful and unexpected reunion on Peary's forty-sixth birthday. As explorers judge their ages he was no longer a young man, but he had work to do and he meant to do it.

That winter was an unusually trying one. At times, even Peary's Eskimo friends seemed to lose faith in him. Some of them became ill, and six of them died. The Eskimos claimed the Almighty Devil was against them because they had agreed to go across the sea ice with Peary.

In the summer of 1901 Mrs. Peary and Ahnighito went south on the supply ship, and Peary again began to move supplies toward the north. His food was bulky and heavy, for he did not have the special condensed food called pemmican which he used later. All that fall and winter he worked.

He was far down the coast from the Polar Sea, near Cape Sabine, and he must travel a long way to reach a point from which he could push out on the sea ice.

It is time to explain what this sea is like.

The Polar Sea is a large ice-covered sea at the top of the world. There are many currents and tides in it. Where Peary wanted to go north the tide is mostly from the west to the east, and somewhat to the south, toward Greenland.

Ice forms on the sea in great cakes, sometimes so many miles in extent that one can travel on these great cakes for days. Sometimes the ice is broken and shifts rapidly, in which case it is very dangerous.

Stretches of water open up, so wide that they are impossible to cross, and the traveler must wait until the "lead," as an opening is called, closes and makes a solid path again. Sometimes it doesn't close.

Nowadays airplanes fly over the northern ice regularly. They go to the North Pole about twice a week. But when Peary was making the trip there were no airplanes. Men went on foot or were towed by their dogs.

Peary started out again in March, 1902, hoping to reach the sea ice before it broke up too much. The journey to Cape Hecla at the top of Grant Land was difficult, and two men nearly lost their lives when they slipped over a fifty-foot ice cliff.

At Hecla, Peary sent back some of the Eskimos, keeping with him four others, and Henson, the colored man. These five were men on whom he could depend. Already he had covered 400 miles of the distance to the edge of the Polar Sea, where he was to make his start for the pole.

The first week in April he went north. This was

much too late in the season, for the ice was ready to shift, and was breaking up. Peary realized this, but he intended to go as far as he could. His feet were in fair condition.

During the first part of the distance to the pole, 450 miles away, the explorers traveled in soft snow and met storms. It was the kind of travel that exhausts both men and animals.

When they at last saw open water ahead, Peary was forced to go farther and farther west to get around it. He finally met what he came to call the "Big Lead," the open water which had stopped him when he tried to go north from Greenland.

After a time the lead began to close, and Peary and his men went across. But on the other side they found smashed ice and more open water. Finally they were forced to stop. They could not go any farther that year if they wished to return; they would be cut off by water behind them.

It was the highest point north that man had ever reached from America—84 degrees, 17 minutes and 27 seconds of latitude. It was farther than Peary had gone from the tip of Greenland.

But he had to stop and go back. There was nothing else to do. He was heartbroken and, for the time being, defeated. Peary did not often get downhearted, but of this setback he wrote:

"The game is off. My dream of sixteen years is

ended. I have made the best fight I knew. I believe it has been a good one. But I cannot accomplish the impossible."

How wrong he was! All these years he had been learning how to meet the north. He *could* do the seemingly impossible, and he was to prove it.

7

THE years of striving that Peary had spent in the north had been directed to a single purpose. He had tried to get to the North Pole through Greenland, and up from the side of Grant Land. And he had failed.

But those years had not been without value, for Peary had learned something important: There was no way to reach the pole except from a ship based on the shore of the Polar Sea. Only one ship had been there before, but Peary decided that anything that had been done once, he could do again.

The only trouble was that there was no ship in existence that suited his purposes. Such a vessel must be able to ram, smash and break its way through ice; it must be able to stand the pressure of ice and pop out of it, the way one would force a ball up between one's hands.

The only way he could get such a ship was to build it, and he had very little money.

When Peary came back from his 1902 trip toward the pole he returned to the Navy Department. After passing two examinations, he became a Commander in the Navy and did some good work in engineering. But those in the department paid little attention to him. He had been away a long time, and he had failed in what he had tried to do.

Men only pay a great deal of attention to spectacular success. That is rather foolish because success takes many forms. A rather modest man may be very successful in ways that do not attract attention, but Peary had been trying to do the spectacular.

At that time, therefore, Peary was no hero, even though he had risked his life many times, and pushed the flag farther north than anyone else.

But while he had been away some good friends who did believe in him had formed the Peary Arctic Club. They had money and offered to raise half the sum necessary to build the ship if Peary would raise the other half. By appeals to many other men and by lectures and books, Peary did manage to get the money together. And into the shipbuilding fund went every cent he had.

He designed the vessel himself. She was to be made of wood to withstand the ice, with steam for bucking the ice and with auxiliary sails. Her bow was slanted so that she could ride up on the ice and crush it by her weight or split it. The crew's quarters were on deck, and all the space below was used for coal and supplies.

The ship was called the *Roosevelt*, after the scrappy and courageous man who was the twenty-sixth President of the United States—Theodore Roosevelt. (This was an appropriate move, for Roosevelt himself became an explorer. After his years as President, he discovered a river in South America, which is named for him. It is in the almost unknown Mato Grosso, in central South America.)

The weather was very hot when Peary sailed from New York in July, 1905.

"We are going to put her right out into the Polar Sea," he said when he left aboard the *Roosevelt*.

His captain, Bob Bartlett, knew how the ice poured into Kane Basin and into Robeson and Kennedy Channels—the passages between Greenland and Grinnell and Grant Land.

"It might be done some years, Commander," said Bob, "but we can't be sure. You know that ice."

Peary looked stern, and his lips tightened. "We are going to do it this year, Bob," he said.

As Bob Bartlett said later, after bucking the ice: "I shouldn't think he would have wanted to see that land again."

And Bartlett was not a man easily daunted. He was short and powerful, with huge arms and a pugnacious jaw. I wrote a story about Bob once, telling how he almost got to the pole before he had to turn back, and he was so pleased with it that he gave me a hug. My ribs almost cracked.

It was an open year up as far as Inglefield Gulf, on the west coast of Greenland. By the time he got there Peary had picked up some of the Eskimos who were going north with him.

An Eskimo settlement is an interesting place. It is odd to stop at a point where black cliffs tower overhead, where the glaciers may come down to the sea, and where the icy rim of the interior shows white over the mountains that hold back masses of snow.

Near the shore there may be a few scattered tents or huts, with men and women in fur clothing standing around shyly, dogs barking and running about, and small Eskimo children looking out from behind their parents. It may be a fairly smelly spot, for Eskimos do not wash, and their huts are none too clean.

From coast-dwelling people such as these, Peary

selected his Eskimos, who joined the expedition along with their wives, children, and dogs. They added considerably to the number of passengers already aboard the little *Roosevelt,* which was only 184 feet long and about 35 feet wide. A count of heads showed a total of forty Eskimos, twenty crewmen, and two hundred dogs.

Then there were tons of walrus and whale meat. Much of the meat was hung in the rigging. What with the yelping dogs, the chattering Eskimos, and the meat, the ship smelled to high heaven. There was noise and confusion. But above it all were the good nature and tolerance of a man who knew he would have to live with these inconveniences for a long time.

The troubles of the ship in the ice had just begun. From Etah north it was a struggle. As soon as the *Roosevelt* pushed out into Smith Sound, she met the heavy pack ice that was rushing down from the north. The ship was lying deep in the water, and Bartlett hesitated at first to ram her into the ice at full speed.

Peary, however, said he would be responsible for whatever might happen, and Bob let her go. She rammed and turned and twisted in the ice, and split floes.

Peary worked his way over to the west side of the lower end of Kane Basin, a big opening between

Greenland and Grinnell Land, and set ashore some stores and coal. Then he rammed and forced his way up the shore, where he had often found open water.

But that year the ice was firmly packed, and Peary decided, against all the rules of northern sea travel, to head over again toward Greenland. (Generally the ice is more open toward Grinnell Land, and more tightly packed on the Greenland shore, but that year the easterly passage seemed best.)

The ice in the channel was heavy at times, and rose high above the sides of the ship. Peary got into the main rigging, and Bartlett and the mate went

up in the foremast rigging. Hanging there, the three men guided the ship.

The masts swayed with the heavy jars against the ice, and the ship slipped from one side to the other as she slid off the ice floes. She backed off and whacked her way forward again, and after hours of ramming what seemed almost solid pack ice she came out into loose ice off the Greenland coast and turned north.

On one occasion the ice, driven by the current, swept the *Roosevelt* aside with such force that her rudder was smashed and her steering gear almost disabled.

After the rudder had been repaired the *Roosevelt* was again shoved out into the ice and forced north. Once she was squeezed so heavily that she rose high out of the water.

"In all my experiences," wrote Peary, "I recall nothing more exciting than the thrill, the crash, the shock of hurling the *Roosevelt,* a fifteen-hundred-ton battering-ram, at the ice to smash a way through."

Again Peary changed his course. He had seen open water on the other side, near Grant Land, and it was not far away.

But between the *Roosevelt* and the open water lay the ice. From Greenland to the other side of the channel it was almost solid and rushing down from the polar sea at a tremendous rate.

For a day and a half Peary forced his ship into this battering and moving mass. She fought and shoved and ran her ironclad bow up onto the ice, splitting it and crushing it. She was like a live thing, fighting every minute of the time. She trembled with the force of the pressure on her and bounced back from the sheer blue ice.

High in the rigging Peary watched her, while up in the crow's nest Bartlett looked for weak spots ahead.

He jumped up and down and yelled in the excitement of the battle, for Bartlett was an excitable man. Peary could hear him yelling to the ship:

"Give it to 'em, *Teddy*, give it to 'em!"

Sometimes a stoker, black from the coal he had been heaving into the fires under the boilers, would come on deck for a breath of fresh air. He'd look over the side at the ice, and growl, "She's got to go through," and then drop down below to heave some more coal.

Peary wrote in his journal:

"I do not think there is another ship afloat that would have survived the ordeal."

But she got to the other side, was caught and shoved aground, got off, and moved north. At last she reached Cape Sheridan, on the northern coast, and there she was caught once more.

The ice came in and hit her hard. The deck bulged up as her sides were squeezed in, the rigging hung loose, the whole ship shivered and groaned. Her ribs cracked until it sounded as if rifles were going off.

And then the tide turned, and the ship settled down. She did not float freely again until the following year.

But she was there, and Peary had won his northern base. It had taken him a month and a half to get there.

8

CAPE SHERIDAN, where the ship rested against the ice, was not a safe spot. But there the *Roosevelt* lay, pointed north but held fast.

Peary did not worry much about her. His first effort was to put essential food and supplies ashore, so that if anything happened to the ship he would have them.

While men slid boxes and crates down the planks to the shore, other men went off hunting for musk oxen and caribou.

The boxes were used to build the walls of huts, in

which everybody could live if the need arose. However, it turned out that most of the crew and Eskimos were satisfied to make their homes on the ship. The Eskimos lived below deck where the stores had been.

After a time men came back with meat. They had also found some snow-white caribou, which Peary called reindeer. These beautiful animals had never been seen before, and some were eventually brought back to the United States.

The dogs made their homes on the coarse gravel around the ship, which they found much more suitable than the wet decks. Then suddenly they began to get sick and die.

It was found that the whale meat which Peary had brought north to feed them had become spoiled. As a result the dogs were poisoned. He had to throw away tons of food, and rely entirely on meat brought in by the hunters.

Most of this meat came from musk oxen. These huge creatures, with large heads and horns, live in the north by eating moss and grass that crop up around rocks which are free of snow. Sometimes the animals dig through the snow to get at it.

When they are attacked they huddle in a circle, with their horns out. They can be dangerous enemies to unarmed men.

It is strange that in those far northern lands there should be musk oxen, caribou and Arctic hares. Not many creatures could survive where there are snow and ice all the year, where it is dark most of the time, and where fierce gales and blizzards threaten every living thing.

All that winter the hunting parties were out. Peary was the first man to go on winter trips, when there is no sun for months. He and his hunters were reasonably warm and safe inside their fur clothing.

All this time men and women were also working on the ship, making sledges, harness for the dogs, tents and fur clothing. They also packed pemmican, a condensed food which is lighter to carry on the trail. Peary made some stoves, heated by alcohol, with which to melt snow for cooking.

It was once so cold on the trail that the alcohol froze almost solid and would not vaporize and light. Peary got it to light by putting a piece of flaming paper on the alcohol.

The winter was a happy one. All hands were kept busy and got along well together, and there were no quarrels. The long, dark winter, with its cold and endless storms, is a bad time, and unless hands are busy, men are apt to brood and become sullen. Work helps to pass the time.

A baby Eskimo, who was born that January, probably holds the record for having arrived farther north than any other infant in history.

In the midst of the camp activity, Peary went

ahead with his plans. He was going to the west, to Cape Hecla, before starting out on the ice.

This time he was going to try shuttling his provisions and fuel over the sea ice to a base camp, from which he could make a final dash for the pole. His plan would succeed only if parties taking the food forward were not shut off from other parties by leads of open water.

There was also the danger that open water between the huge shifting floes might cut off some men trying to return to land. If this happened, those farthest from land might have great difficulty in getting back or might not be able to get back at all.

The colored man, Henson, was selected to make the trail because of his skill as a dog driver. His sledges were light and he could travel fast. Then came the others.

The sun shone for a few minutes on the horizon as Peary started. It was about the middle of February, 1906.

At the end of each march, Henson made an igloo of snow, which was used by the others who followed him. In turn, they also made igloos. The ice was in continuous motion. It would split and the resulting cakes would slide over each other. Now and then the ice broke under the igloos, smashing them, too, but they could usually be repaired.

Sometimes the crash of breaking ice was like an

earthquake, and the frightened Eskimos would run outdoors to see what had happened.

The marches went steadily forward, often through heavy snow over the ice, and always on ice that shifted to the east. It was more than fifty and sixty degrees below zero, and the work was desperately hard. Henson often had to build night shelters for the dogs to keep the wind from them.

The party crossed many places where there had been open water as the ice moved, but it was so cold that new ice had formed quickly.

Things were going so smoothly, however, that Peary was beginning to think he might succeed, and he did not like to stop even for rest at night. Always he was aware of the danger of open water ahead of or behind him.

He must hurry while the cold weather lasted.

And then he met his first serious delay.

Far ahead of him he saw some dark objects, and when he came up to them they proved to be three of his sledging parties which had been stopped by open water. He could not see across, and later he learned that the lead was more than two miles wide.

It was the Big Lead, and he called it the "Hudson River." He could not pass it.

Men were sent out to the east and the west, to try to find a way across the lead, but they reported that the open space was widening. For days the explorers hunted for a crossing, and although the water froze some distance from the edges of the lead, there was still an open place in the center. But this finally closed also, and Peary could send across light sledges.

But the weather had changed once more, with heavy wind and an overcast sky. In the northern regions, traveling can be very peculiar when the sun is not shining. There are no shadows, for there is nothing but snow and ice. There is nothing on which to focus the eyes except the sledges or the dogs.

The result is—and I have experienced it—that one cannot see the surface on which he is walking. The surface can be felt; it is hard and solid; but it cannot be seen, and the sensation is like walking on nothing. I have seen an experienced skier stumble over a little ridge of snow in front of him which he could not see. It is very easy to get snow blindness under such conditions, for the eyes strain to fasten on something.

When the travelers stopped, the wind howled louder outside their igloos, and the snow fell, much of it drift that had been picked up by the wind. Huddled in his igloo, Peary wondered what the storm would be like at the Big Lead; perhaps it had opened up again so that men could not come up with supplies.

He called this stopping-place Storm Camp, for he was held there for six days. Several times he tried to go out in the blinding drift and freezing wind, but as it was fifty below zero he soon found that nobody, not even he, could travel in such weather.

And all the time the ice was drifting him to the east of the route he wanted to follow.

When the weather cleared he sent men back to see what had happened to the supporting parties, but the messengers soon returned with news that the lead had opened. The open water would now prevent any more supplies from reaching Peary and his party.

There was nothing to do except go on with what supplies they had, much too small a quantity for the eight men. Peary traveled fast while he could, and in a few marches he made thirty to forty miles a day.

Some dogs gave out under the pace that was set, for there was not enough food to give them strength. The dogs that dropped were fed to the others.

Finally Peary reached 87 degrees, 6 minutes north latitude. He could go no farther without starving to death on the way home.

"As I looked at the drawn faces of my comrades," he wrote, "at the skeleton figures of my few remaining dogs, at my nearly emptied sledges, and remembered the drifting ice over which we had come and the unknown quantity of the 'big lead' between us and the nearest land, I felt that I had cut the margin as narrow as could reasonably be expected."

So he turned back in April, only 170-odd miles from the pole. Again he had failed to make it.

"WILL WE GET BACK?"

9

THE return trip to land was one of Peary's most difficult journeys. It nearly cost him his life.

The bitter, needle-like wind was still blowing and cut the men's faces as they headed into it. When they stumbled into camp that night Peary was exhausted and nearly blind from the effects of the snow and wind.

And he was on the sea, the drifting ice, unable to see through the storm ahead. Added to the other miseries was the distressing thought that he and his men were more than 250 miles from land where there was food.

He had to cover his eyes with snow for hours until they were numb. Finally the pain died down, and he was able to sleep.

Day after day the party struggled on, until at last they came back to Storm Camp. There another blizzard met them, and the igloos were found half full of snow.

The explorers had now drifted so far to the east that Peary set a course as straight as he could for the tip of Greenland, instead of Cape Hecla to the west. The Eskimos thought he was wrong. They were sure they had drifted west.

When they reached the Big Lead there was no water. Only the broken and shattered ice showed where the two edges of the pack had ground together before freezing into a solid mass.

At another lead, where new ice had formed, they tried to cross, but the ice bent under them and they had to scramble back. Again they reached a large lead, which they crossed on snowshoes to distribute their weight, and the ice bent under them. They were afraid one of them might go through. That dangerous spot was two miles wide. But they had to cross it.

"Frankly I do not care for more similar experiences," Peary said.

Once the toes of his snowshoes went through the ice and almost tripped him. If he had fallen he would have drowned. Nobody could have helped him. Just after he and his men had passed, the ice opened again.

At last they saw the snow-topped hills of Greenland in the distance. Encouraged by the sight, they passed to solid ice protected by the land, and by luck picked up one of the other parties which was headed the wrong way, away from the ship. The men of this party were weak and dazed from lack of food, and would have died in a short time if they had not been found.

Peary's food was almost gone, but he thought he knew where musk oxen could be found. When one of the Eskimos sighted some, six miles away, Peary and a few of his men started running for them, stumbling and exhausted from hunger.

Two of the dogs were sent ahead to round up the

oxen, but one of the thin dogs got too close and was tossed in the air. The other, his legs bending under him from weakness, kept up the attack.

At last Peary was near enough to the animals to shoot. He was so excited and worn out that he had to sit down on the snow a minute to pull himself together. Then he lifted himself to his feet and sighted.

One by one he got them all. The Eskimos cut off huge pieces of the meat, and dogs and men ate the raw food until they dared not eat more.

It had been a close call. For two days and nights they slept and ate musk oxen, cooked over a tiny fire, until everyone was partially restored to strength.

That trip back over the northern shore of Greenland was one of the hardest marches ever made. The men ate hare and whatever else they could find.

But they reached the *Roosevelt* and sent men back to help two or three who were too lame or too weak to come on by themselves. Peary was almost snow-blind.

Ootah, an Eskimo dog driver, threw himself down, and sighed:

"I have got back again, thank God."

But Peary, who never seemed too tired to travel, no sooner got back than he went to the west to dis-

cover new land. This he accomplished after a sledging trip of 600 miles in fifty-eight days, often wading through water.

10

GETTING the *Roosevelt* south from Grant Land was little short of a miracle, for everything seemed to have gone wrong. On the way north two boilers had blown up, but luckily nobody was killed. Then whale oil from the meat seeped through the timbers. An Eskimo carelessly knocked out a pipe on deck and the ship caught fire.

While Peary was still in west Grant Land the ship had been beset by millions of tons of ice. Or so it seemed to Bob Bartlett, the captain. She had been pinched against the land by the pack, and to save her Bartlett had used some dynamite. In his excitement he had used too much, and the ship had been damaged aft.

Outside Cape Sheridan the ice pack kept moving up and down the coast. Frequently the *Roosevelt* was pinched so hard that she rose out of the water. One of these jams sheered two blades from her propeller, and ripped the rudder post loose.

After one of the worst jams Bartlett ran down into the hold, and found a big hole in the bottom of the ship. He could see through it, and thought it was big enough for a boy to crawl through.

He filled the hole with cement and anything else he could lay his hands on. The pumps were started and forced much of the water out of the ship. But then a new danger threatened. The weather changed and it began to blow and snow. However, all hands worked, because only in that way could they be sure of getting back.

A few days later Peary came back to the ship, a lonesome figure, limping ahead of his Eskimos. While he slept the others kept on making a new rudder.

Rested at last, Peary came on deck and talked to Bartlett about the ship. Then he went down, and after looking at the hole in the bottom, turned to Bob and said:

"We have got to get her back, Captain. We are going to come back next year."

Bartlett looked at him in amazement.

The coal was shifted forward and the new rudder forced down.

There seemed to be some clear water beyond the pack near the shore, so despite the gale that was blowing, Bartlett got up steam and headed out. They came out of Kennedy Channel and went down through Kane Basin. It was so choked with ice that they could do nothing but drift.

Ice poked the cement out of the hole in the bottom, and two men were stationed there to make sure that the hole was filled again as soon as water began pouring in. The ice was so bad it did not seem possible that they would be able to work south.

Late in August Peary went to Bartlett and said:

"Captain, I give us three days more. By that time either the ship will be out, or we will have to winter here."

"Well," said Bartlett, "then we better get some musk oxen. They taste good."

For seventy-five days they made their way by inches in a sinking ship from Cape Sheridan to Etah, Greenland.

There they were able to beach the ship stern first at high tide. When the tide went down they looked over the damage.

The jury rudder—the one they had made to take the place of the regular rudder—was smashed to bits. The two remaining propeller blades were bent and cracked. All around the largest hole in the bottom the wood was splintered.

When Bartlett saw what had happened he was as willing to believe that he could walk home as that he could sail there in the *Roosevelt*.

And then Peary sent for him. "Captain," he said, "we've got to hurry now. The nights are getting dark."

Bob almost laughed. But then he caught something of Peary's spirit. They would get out of there! "All right," said he, "all sleep is out until we fix her."

And fix her they did. They patched up the propeller and tightened up the nuts. They straightened the plates and patched up the hole in the bottom. They did the seemingly impossible, there on the shore of that bleak cold inlet, although they didn't know how long the bottom would last.

Then they steamed down to Etah fjord where the coal had been left when they went north. It was partly frozen, and had to be dynamited before they could get it aboard.

Started down the coast again, they went in close to shore to drop some Eskimos. Here misfortune again beset them and they ran aground. There was only one propeller blade left now, and at low tide they discovered that it was loose. If it had dropped off they would have been done for in the ice, for they could not turn quickly under sail.

Men went overboard in the icy water and tightened up the last propeller blade.

When they got down to Cape York more hard luck awaited them. Storms of more than fifty miles an hour do not often occur in the north, but at this time a severe one came up.

Peary described it only as a fresh breeze, but Bartlett, who was a good seafaring man, said it was a "humdinger."

Water got into the hold, and ashes clogged the pumps, so that the water rose rapidly. Men went down into the dirty water, which often sloshed over their heads, and cut holes through the seven-inch-thick after bulkhead. This permitted the water to get to the main pumps.

Often during this time, when Bartlett was not sure that the ship would survive, Peary kept talking about his plans for the next trip!

They ran into gale after gale, steering largely with sails and traveling fast in the high wind.

Finally the third rudder was carried away. Then the foretopmast went over the side with a crash, taking the rigging with it. They dropped the end of the main boom overboard to act as a jury rudder, and carried on.

A fourth rudder was made when the wind went down a little, and with the aid of all hands it was fastened on the bobbing ship so that it would work after a fashion.

Slowly they worked their way down the Labrador coast, putting in at little harbors for wood, and lashing the ship against the gale to the rocks on the shore.

At Sydney, Nova Scotia, they took on coal, and on Christmas Eve the ship dropped anchor in the North River at New York.

Safe in home waters, Peary gripped Bartlett's hand, but did not say a word.

Later Admiral Sigsbee, who was in command of

the *Maine* when she was blown up, called this trip "one of the ablest, most resourceful and courageous affairs of its kind in the annals of Arctic exploration."

11

IN 1908 when Peary went north on what he knew would be his last trip, he was fifty-two years old. For more than twenty years he had been trying to reach the North Pole. Only a succession of gales that kept open wide stretches of water had prevented him from getting there two years before.

Before the *Roosevelt* started out again she put in at Oyster Bay, Long Island, where President Theodore Roosevelt came aboard to look over the staunch ship named for him.

"Mr. President, I shall put into this everything

72

there is in me—physical, mental, and moral," said Peary, as the President went over the rail.

"I believe in you, Peary," replied the President, "and I believe in your success—if it is within the possibility of man."

They shook hands, and Peary turned his little ship toward the sea.

It went north to Cape York in Greenland, where the Eskimos came out in their kayaks, or skin canoes, to wave at their old friend.

"The natives were overjoyed to see Peary again," said Bob Bartlett. "Each time I went north it was a revelation to me how they loved the big white man who came to them year after year, treating them like a father, and always leaving with them gifts of priceless value."

For a gun was priceless to an Eskimo.

By the time Peary reached Etah he had taken aboard all the dogs and Eskimos he needed. And when he left there he wrote:

"Behind me now lay everything that was mine, everything that a man personally loves, family, friends, home, and all those kindred associations that linked me with my kind.

"Ahead of me lay my dream, my destiny, the goal of that irresistible impulse which had driven me for twenty-three years to hurl myself, time after time, against the frigid *NO* of the Great North.

"The life is a dog's life, but the work is a man's work."

As usual the ship was crowded to the limit, and even the stoical Bartlett was affected by it.

"To my dying day," he wrote, "I shall never forget the frightful noise, the choking stench, and the terrible confusion."

Despite the confusion, the *Roosevelt* was forced through the terrible ice between Greenland and Grant Land, and finally was anchored safely at Cape Sheridan. Her gracefully curved and steel-clad bow had split and rammed its way again to within 450 miles of the pole.

At Cape Sheridan some Eskimos hunted, while others worked on the sledges. Peary's sledges, which he was always improving, were made particularly for the rough work over smashed ice in the north. They were very strong and had steel runners. Each carried about 650 pounds of supplies, of which about 500 pounds was food for the dogs.

These small and sturdy animals were hitched fan-wise, so that they spread out in front of the sledge, each dog pulling on his own single trace. It was the best way for broken ice, but when the traces got mixed up they were difficult for bare hands to untangle at a temperature of fifty degrees below zero.

There were three sledges and three men in each unit, for three men could haul a sledge over heaped-

up pressure ridges or out of holes. At these times, of course, the dogs sat down and looked as if they were laughing. The men were doing the work.

Peary was to start this time from Cape Columbia, some distance farther west than he had started before, to allow for the eastward drift of the ice. Before winter set in, nearly all supplies for the trip had been hauled up to the cape.

While this was going on Peary went off on a mere jaunt, a 200-mile sledge trip to explore a deep inlet!

The Eskimos were a little nervous about the coming journey, for they knew how difficult and dangerous the others had been. So in February Peary called them together and spread on a table before them rifles, shotguns, ammunition, knives, and other things. Then he announced that each man who went north with him could also have a tent and a boat.

At once their desire to make the trip increased.

Peary's plan this time was to have a number of supporting parties shuttling back and forth on the trail, each bringing up supplies. The object was to place the Commander about 150 miles from the pole, with full loads, and the best of the dogs. This would greatly increase his chance of success.

The hardest work would fall on the party which went ahead to break trail and to find ways through the ice. This party would also have to leave a well-marked track over which Peary would follow.

When the party got together at Cape Columbia ready to start it was a very cold day—too cold for the new men who had not entirely learned to protect themselves. Two or three of them were surprised at Peary's announcement that their noses or cheeks were frozen. They had not known it. (Strangely enough, when a part of your body freezes you are not apt to feel it, but when it thaws out it hurts, badly.)

"How cold is it?" the men asked.

"Oh, about fifty-seven below," Peary said.

The night before they left, some of the men got together with Captain Bartlett in a tent, and sang songs and gave college cheers. Among the merry-makers were George Borup, a youngster who had been a track star at Yale and whom everybody liked for his good nature; Donald MacMillan, who has since gone north many times; and Ross Marvin, a college instructor, who had been north on the previous trip. Bob said he could make as much noise as these young fellows, but that his noise wasn't organized.

Then they all shook hands, and Bartlett remarked:

"When you say good-by to a fellow here, the Lord knows when you'll meet him again."

(It was to be the last trip for Marvin. He never did get back.)

That same night Peary got them all around him for his final instructions. As Borup said:

"It reminded me somewhat of the way a football team gathers around its leader just before trotting out on the field before a big game. He told us he wasn't a believer in hot air, but in action. He also said the next six weeks were going to be undiluted misery, the only variation in the monotony being that occasionally it would get worse."

On February 28, 1909, Bartlett started north, and day after day the others followed him. They carried their loads forward, dropped them, and turned back. They picked up other supplies and raced forward again to join the slower trail breakers.

The entire group now came up to the Big Lead, the "Hudson River," as Peary called it, and were stuck for five days. But they kept going, a team dropping out now and then so that it would not eat too far into the supplies. At last only Peary and Bartlett and Henson were left.

When they had almost reached 88 degrees north latitude Bartlett turned back. Before he left Peary he walked five miles farther north, hoping to reach 88 degrees, but he was not successful.

Bartlett has told me about that walk. After he was out of sight of Peary, and at the end of his farthest northern march, he put down two flags on the trail. I believe they were the flags of Newfoundland and of England. (Bob came from Newfoundland.)

And then he knelt beside the flags in the snow for a few minutes and prayed. When he rose, he carefully wrapped up the flags and walked back to Peary.

Although Bartlett wanted to go on, he said nothing about it, for he knew that Henson was the better dog driver. Bartlett realized, too, that he was needed to guide his Eskimos back to the land.

Before Peary started on his last march, he picked out the best dogs for the northward dash. It was 137 miles to the pole. He and Henson had forty dogs, four Eskimos, and plenty of supplies. Peary himself was in good condition. And the ice was better than it had been for a long time.

"It looked like a boulevard before him," Bartlett told me years later.

"Good-by, Captain," Peary said to Bartlett. "Take care of yourself. Watch out for young ice. Clean up the ship when you get back. Don't worry about me. I'll be back."

But Bob Bartlett knew Peary wouldn't be back unless he made it. This was to be his last trip and he was determined to succeed.

"If we get there," said Peary, "it will be the South Pole next and you as leader."

12

IN MANY ways Peary's last trip, the journey to the pole, was the easiest he had ever made, for this time luck was with him.

Always in the back of his mind was the Big Lead, that opening of water that might cut him off from the land. But this year he was earlier than usual, ice conditions were better, and he had the experience of having passed the Big Lead once before.

Perhaps it could be passed again. But he was going a lot farther from land.

Before starting, he put the sledges and gear into

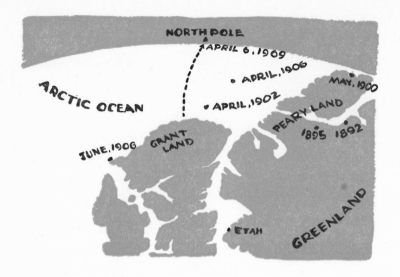

perfect condition. Soon after midnight of April 2 he began the journey. He could see easily, for the sun was up all the twenty-four hours of the day. It was not far above the horizon, but enough.

Peary made it a rule to walk some distance alone before the sledge caught up with him, so that his legs and feet would remain in good condition. He did this on his last dash to the pole. Part of the time he rode on the sledge, but as he approached the end of the day's march he always got off and walked.

So he went into the lead for this last lap as he wanted to. As he strode along he recalled his other trips north; he thought of the many years, before his feet had been injured, when he could stride along thirty or forty miles a day on snowshoes.

The years dropped from him as he headed straight for his goal.

He was fifty-three years old now, but still tall, powerful, and easily the strongest man in his party. Only a man of strength and endurance could attempt the journey which he had just begun.

Coming to a lead, he picked his way across on moving ice cakes, finding a way for the dogs and sledges to follow him. He coaxed the dogs to jump some of the narrower stretches of water.

There were rough places in the ice, but not so bad as they had been before. Even the Eskimos began to be excited, as they realized they were nearing the end of their journey.

On one of the leads they crossed, the ice was so thin that it bent under their weight. The last two men went over on hands and knees, letting the dogs and sledges go ahead.

The day before they reached the pole, the sky became overcast, and everything around them was bathed in a gray light that cast no shadows. It was like traveling in a bowl of milk. And it was depressing. But Peary pushed on so rapidly that in twelve hours he made thirty miles.

On April 6, when he ended his last march, he knew he was within a short distance of the pole, but he was too tired to move. His life's purpose had been accomplished, but he was too weary to appreciate it.

Igloos were made and the party turned in for a few hours of sleep.

Then Peary awoke and started out again. When he took observations of the sun with his sextant and artificial horizon, they showed that he was beyond the pole. He had done what he set out to do.

He had reached the North Pole on April 6, 1909.

He found it hard to realize that for the first few hours of that march he had been going north, and for the last part of it he had been going south. The tiny mathematical point that he had sought was somewhere near him. He marched in several directions and took many observations of the sun to prove his position. When he was through he knew that somewhere he had come very close to the place that he had sought.

The American flag was raised over a block of ice, and a few other flags, such as those of his fraternity and college, were also planted. The Eskimos cheered. A bottle with a record in it was buried in the snow.

Thirty hours were spent at the pole, and then Peary wrote a little note to his wife from the top of the world. .

At last the party left, and started back for Cape Columbia. As they marched, Peary wondered if they would ever reach it. Would he ever have the chance to tell the world of what he had done?

The journey back was fairly easy, compared to

the return from the previous trip. They struck leads, but managed to get across. On April 22 they reached Grant Land safely.

The Eskimos sang and danced with delight. As Ootah sank down on his sledge he said:

"The Devil is asleep or having trouble with his wife, or we never should have come back so easily."

Peary had lost thirty pounds on the trip. He was haggard, but delighted with his success. When he reached the ship Bartlett ran up to him, grasped his hand, and congratulated him.

"How did you know?" asked Peary, with a smile.

There was bad news awaiting him, however, for the others told him that Marvin, the college instructor, had fallen into a lead on the way home and been drowned. It was not until years later that the truth came out. One of the Eskimos confessed that he had thought Marvin was about to injure his companion, and had shot him.

The return could not begin until summer warmth had weakened the ice. The ship finally got away from Cape Sheridan on July 18, and eventually reached New York.

For his accomplishment Peary, the greatest of our polar explorers, was made a Rear Admiral in the Navy, and received many honors in this country and abroad.

PART TWO

The South Pole

13

THE Arctic and the Antarctic are alike in only one respect: they are both cold. And the Antarctic is a little colder than the Arctic.

This is because the Arctic around the pole is at sea level; it is a sea surrounded by land. The Antarctic is a high land, reaching up to more than 9,000 feet at the pole. This great altitude makes it very cold.

Only around the edges in summer is the Antarctic above freezing. How cold it becomes in the interior nobody knows, for nobody has ever been at the South

Pole in the winter time. But it must be the coldest place in the world.

At times it is almost as cold in the winter in the northern parts of the United States as in the Antarctic—as much as 60 below zero. And in Siberia it often gets down to 90 below zero.

But the unusual thing about the Antarctic is that the cold there lasts for a long time. I remember when I was there it averaged more than 44 below zero for two whole months. That is cold! And the coldest we had was nearly 73 below zero. It was probably more than 90 below zero at the pole.

The Arctic and the Antarctic differ in another way.

In the Arctic there are polar bears and Eskimos.

The only living things in the Antarctic in the winter time are a few large Emperor penguins. There are no seals, no other birds.

Even in the summer time there are only a few seals and whales on the edges of the continent and some birds, including penguins. Nothing else lives in the Antarctic except a few explorers who go there for a short time. And there are no polar bears.

It is a dead land, covered with ice and snow and with high mountains. Men who go there cannot get out except for a few months in the summer, for it is surrounded by ice.

It is odd, but never explained, that the earth is pushed in at the North Pole to make a sea 14,000 feet deep. And it bulges out at the South Pole to make a high plateau of 9,000 feet. It is as if somebody hit the earth with a big fist. Why? Nobody knows.

As most of the Antarctic is on land or is ice held in by land, traveling there is very different from what it is in the Arctic. When one goes out on the Arctic sea ice, one never knows where the ice will drift. But in the Antarctic a man can go into the interior and know that his path will remain until he comes back.

The Antarctic is a big place. It is larger than the United States and Mexico, with part of Canada thrown in for good measure. Once upon a time it was warm, for coal is found there, and coal is made from old buried trees and plants.

Some of the outlines of these trees and ferns of long ago have been found in the Antarctic coal beds. But nobody has found the remains of any animal that ever lived there.

The penguins must have been Antarctic birds who could fly when the country was warmer, but their wings now have no feathers. They are only tough bits of gristle that the penguin uses for swimming.

A man can wonder about the Antarctic for a long time. Men did—as men always wonder about the unknown—and started to poke into it, trying to get through the ice that surrounded it.

There are only two good ways to get into the interior. One of them was found by a daring Englishman, Sir James Clark Ross. He shoved his old sailing ships into a belt of pack ice south of New Zealand, managed to work them through the ice, and found himself in a big body of water with little ice in it.

He started to sail south, thinking he might be able to sail to the pole, but he found himself stopped by a wall of ice 400 miles long. It was from 50 to 200 feet high, and to this day it is known as the Ross Barrier, or ice shelf.

The other entrance to the continent is more dangerous. It is called the Weddell Sea, also named after the Englishman who discovered it. Neither Ross Sea nor Weddell Sea is safe for ships, although the latter is the worse of the two. Whalers work in the Ross Sea, but they have never dared to go far into the Weddell Sea.

Most of the entrances into the Antarctic have been through the Ross Sea, at the east or west end of the great barrier. Almost all the rim of the continent has been seen now, by sea or air, but except for the polar trips men have never gone very far into it.

Two great explorers went to the South Pole within a month of each other. Roald Amundsen, a Norwegian, reached there on December 16, 1911, and Captain Robert Falcon Scott, an Englishman, got there a month later, on January 17, 1912.

There could hardly have been two more different men than Scott and Amundsen. Amundsen was probably the greatest sledge traveler of his time, a swift mover like Peary. He cared little for scientific exploration. He loved the unknown, and looked on it as a challenge. Where men had not been he wanted to go. And he was at home in the Polar Regions.

He had a prominent nose that made him rather sharp-featured. He was broad-shouldered, wiry, hard physically and mentally. Strangely enough, he was a sentimental man. I learned this when I was with him at Spitzbergen before he flew over the North Pole. He used to play a record of "Home, Sweet Home," and listen to it almost with tears in his eyes.

Scott was a shorter, broader man, tough physically, and tenacious. He was a great leader of scientific men, and went deeply into all the problems of his environment. He was emotional and easily moved, but a man who got things done.

Amundsen and Scott used different routes to the

South Pole. Scott went to the east up the great Beardmore Glacier, which was already known, and Amundsen went up the unknown Axel Heiberg Glacier to the west.

Amundsen knew how to handle dogs and he used them for hauling his food and tents. Although he met difficulties, as everyone does who ventures into the Antarctic, he made the pole.

On his return trip he idled in his tent so that he would not get back before he planned to do so, and even threw away some food.

Scott, like most British explorers, did not believe in dogs. He used ponies for part of the trip, but most of his pulling was done by manpower.

He and his companions hitched themselves to the sledges and hauled them up the glacier, across the great plateau, which was over 9,000 feet high. Then he went on to the pole, and down to his last camp. When he had got within eleven miles of the camp, he was snowed in by a blizzard that lasted two weeks.

He could not move. He could not get fuel or food. And with his companions he died, one of the greatest and bravest explorers in history. His last words in his diary were:

"For God's sake look after our people."

When he was found his arm was thrown over the body of his friend, Dr. Edward A. Wilson, who had died earlier.

14

IT WAS into this desolate country that Rear Admiral Richard E. Byrd, then a Commander in the Navy, decided to fly. Men had reached the North and South Poles on foot, but he wanted to be the first to get there by air.

This was difficult, for in the late 1920's airplanes and engines were not as reliable as they are now. There were few instruments. And the Antarctic is torn by quick storms, with few good flying days.

But Byrd's training for his work had been good. He was one of three brothers who came from a well-known Virginia family. One of his ancestors was among the first settlers of Virginia, and a founder of the city of Richmond. A brother, Harry, is a prominent United States Senator, and a former Governor of his State. Another brother, Tom, is one of the foremost apple growers in the country.

Tom, Dick, and Harry!

Dick Byrd, who was born October 25, 1888, wanted to go into the Navy. After completing his studies at Annapolis, where he played football, he joined his ship. But he soon found that an injury to a foot kept him from standing watches. So he had to resign, and it seemed that his chosen career was over.

But during the First World War, flying became so important that Byrd decided to be a pilot. Even if he couldn't stand watches he could at least sit down and fly a plane.

He entered the naval flying school at Pensacola, Florida, and when he passed his tests he was sent to Halifax, Nova Scotia, as commandant of a group of planes. They were to patrol off the coast for submarines.

While Byrd was at Halifax the Navy built its first big flying boat. Dick tried to go with it across the ocean, but the end of the war prevented that flight. When Navy boats did cross he was not with them.

In 1921 Byrd went to England to fly the British dirigible ZR2, a big airship modeled after the German Zeppelins. He missed a train on his way north to join the crew, and someone else took his place at the last moment. The big airship crashed the next day and burned.

Then came his opportunity for air adventure in the north polar region.

Commander Donald MacMillan, who had been with Peary, was going north again in 1925, and hoped to have two Navy airplanes. The amphibian, a plane that can land and take off from either sea or land, had just been invented. Byrd got permission to go as commander of these two planes.

Peary had long anticipated the use of airplanes in the polar regions. So had Byrd, and this was his chance. Up to that time no airplanes had been used in the mountainous northern country that he was to invade.

Where Peary and others had struggled with dog teams, Byrd was to fly, and in a few hours cover distances that had taken Peary many days.

The expedition went up the west coast of Greenland as far as possible by ship. It was not easy to find a stretch of open water that was sufficiently free of ice to permit taking off. But a bay was found just north of Etah, then the northernmost home of the Eskimo.

It was on this trip that Byrd got to know Floyd

Bennett, a naval mechanic and pilot who was to have a great influence on Byrd's life.

Bennett was a man to remember. He was calm, reliable, and possessed of a sterling character. He was a good flier who never got excited, and he could be daring when it was necessary. Floyd Bennett Field in Brooklyn, New York, is named for him. He died in Canada on a trip to rescue some fliers.

Byrd and Bennett made several trips over Grinnell Land, and over the edge of the Greenland ice cap. They confirmed many of Peary's discoveries of land to the west.

That trip with MacMillan turned Byrd's thoughts to the North Pole. Perhaps the flight could be made with the Wright Whirlwind engine (small by pres-

ent standards) which had just been put on the mar-
ket. It was only 220 horsepower, an air-cooled engine,
but it did so well that in a few years it became a
household word.

The plane was available too. Anthony Fokker,
the Hollander who made war planes for the Ger-
mans, had come to this country. The body of his
plane—the fuselage—was covered with canvas,
and the wing was made of wood.

There were three engines, one on each side under
the wing, and one in the nose. We have since
learned that such an arrangement is not efficient,
but for its day, back in 1925 and 1926, it was a
good plane. And it would lift a lot.

Byrd's best place to start was Spitzbergen, where
at King's Bay he would be only 750 miles from the
pole. That was a long flight at that time, and it was
all over drifting ice and water.

I was there when he took off down a little slope,
with Bennett as pilot, and I watched him vanish toward the north. Fifteen hours and thirty minutes
later he returned safely, having reached the pole. It
was a flight that immediately made him known as
one of the world's most famous explorers by air.

Then in 1927 Byrd began to plan for a trans-
atlantic flight. But the plane turned over on a trial
flight and badly injured some of the men in it, including Floyd Bennett. After it was repaired and

was being tested again, air history was being made: a young man named Charles A. Lindbergh flew the ocean alone in thirty-three and a half hours.

However, Byrd finished his tests and hopped off a few days after Lindbergh landed in France. With him were Bert Acosta, Bernt Balchen, who later flew his plane to the South Pole, and George Noville.

They met bad weather, and reached the coast of France in a storm. Unable to see Paris, they turned back to the coast and landed in the sea at Ver-sur-Mer by the light of flares. They were badly shaken up but not injured.

The trip proved that a heavy airplane, a three-motored plane, carrying four men and large quantities of gasoline, could fly the Atlantic. It gave promise of the present-day flights across the ocean by larger planes.

Byrd was now ready for the Antarctic and the difficult flight to the South Pole.

15

AT DUNEDIN, New Zealand, Dick Byrd stood on the deck load of the wooden sailing ship, a barkentine, which was going to take him to the Antarctic.

It was a huge deck load, made up of parts of houses and other material, and topped by crates of snarling, snapping and barking dogs.

It was bedlam. Men scurried around the bark, trying to get last things aboard—a little more food, crates of medical supplies, and all the thousands of things that must be taken on an expedition. One cannot buy anything in the Antarctic.

The men who trundled hand trucks along were tired and red-eyed, clad in the rough clothes they would wear on the 2,300-mile voyage south. Scientists, dog drivers, doctor, ship's crew and volunteers, they all looked disreputable.

The ship was filthy. Byrd, now a Commander in the Navy, trim in shirt and trousers, with an overseas cap on his head, tapped his cigarette in its holder, and looked worried.

Lower and lower sank the ship, until she was well over the Plimsoll mark, the mark which shows the legal depth to which a ship may be loaded. But the Antarctic was not a place for nice legalities.

A Norwegian who had been down south, whaling, came up to shake hands with his friend, Sverre Strom, mate of the ship.

"You'll never make it with that load," he said anxiously. "I've been there and I know."

Strom grinned. "We make it," he said.

The *City of New York* was an unusual vessel. Her ribs were so close together that one could hardly get a hand between them. She was planked heavily inside and out, and over all was a sheathing of greenheart, a tough slippery wood over which ice slides. Her sides were three feet thick.

She had been an old Norwegian sealer, the *Samson*, which Byrd had bought in Norway at Amundsen's suggestion. Amundsen had sailed in her as a young man. She had a rickety old engine, but it worked after a fashion. She could stand lots of pressure.

Her hold was loaded with coal, and her 'tween decks with supplies and an airplane. There had been no place for the furs, so they had been tossed into the cabin aft, and filled it nearly to the ceiling. I went with the expedition to write stories for *The New York Times,* and I slept on those furs most of the way south. They were soft, but smelled.

Byrd had more than the *City of New York* to worry about. He had another ship, the *Eleanor Bolling,* a steel trawler, which carried two airplanes, including the big Ford with which the polar flight was to be made.

Byrd was a good organizer. For months he had been getting material together and planning the way in which it should be sent south.

With the airplane pilots and mechanics, and a few others, he had gone on to San Diego, California, and then, with quantities of stores, had left for Wellington, New Zealand, on the 17,000-ton whaler *Larsen.*

Crammed with supplies, the *City of New York* and the *Eleanor Bolling* had left New York and, after passing through the Panama Canal, reached Dunedin. The men and material from Wellington were brought together also at the docks in Dunedin.

We were now ready to start for our main objective.

Aboard the two ships of the expedition there were eighty-three men, forty-two of whom were to live for a year on the ice. It takes a lot of men to handle three airplanes, the oil and gas needed for them, and hundreds of tons of supplies.

And there were no docks where we were going. Getting stuff out of those ships was going to be a hard job.

Finally Byrd was satisfied that he could not cram another ounce on the *City* without danger.

"Let's go," he said, and the ropes were cast off. Out at sea the *Bolling* took the *City* in tow. And a lot of us wasted no time in getting seasick.

Except for one gale the two ships had an unusually lucky passage. The *Bolling* rolled her rails under, and the *City* rolled badly also, but rode the waves like a duck. She was a good ship, the *City*, even if she was a bit slow.

Once we wirelessed ahead to the *Bolling* that she was doing a lot of rolling, and the answer came back:

"You ought to see yourselves!"

Just before we got to the pack ice, Byrd passed the Scott Islands, the second time on record that they had been seen. They are tiny little islands, mere bits of rock sticking out of a lonely sea, and named for gallant Captain Scott.

When we reached the edge of the pack ice, we found nothing but gloom. The sky was a dirty dark gray, and there was a good deal of fog. Fortunately, the wind was not blowing hard.

Navigation was almost impossible. The compass moved all the time, and sometimes it seemed to turn right around. We were close to the South Magnetic Pole.

With a direction finder, we picked up signals from the *Larsen*. After the *Bolling* had left us and gone north again, we met the *Larsen* in a bay of the ice. The sun came out.

Steam was rising from the *Larsen*, her sides were streaked and dirty, and strips of blubber hung down them to act as buffers.

While we watched, one of her chasers—small boats that are about the size of tugs and used to catch whales—got a whale not more than a mile from us.

Later, some of us went on board the *Larsen* to call on Captain Nilsen. The crew were hauling the whale on deck as we climbed over the side.

That whale was nearly a hundred feet long, and weighed about a ton for every foot. The blue whale, as it is called, is the largest animal that has ever lived on earth.

In a little more than an hour the whale had been cut up and was in the boilers, being turned into oil and fertilizer.

The deck of the *Larsen* was red with slush, and she smelled awful. But we had tea and aquavit in the captain's cabin.

In a day or two the *Larsen* took us in tow and hauled us through the pack. Her powerful engines could split the ice, and if she got stuck the little chasers ran full tilt up on the ice, and broke it around her until she could get started again.

One day we were stuck in the ice while a blizzard raged. From ahead we could hear hammering on the steel side of the whaler as the ice squeezed her. We merely lay still while the wind howled and the snow blew.

It was a gray day, but sometimes a little light would come through a break in the clouds. We could see big, uplifted chunks of ice, or an iceberg. And sometimes a white bird flitted out of the air like a ghost and vanished into the wall of ice around us.

After eight days we came to the south side of the pack, which was 240 miles wide that year. The sun was shining, the air was warm, and the sea was calm.

The *Larsen* cast us loose, and we headed south into a calm inland strip of water that reminded us of Long Island Sound or Chesapeake Bay in the springtime.

It was the Ross Sea.

With the antique engine pounding away below, Byrd set course for the barrier, and just before mid-

night on Christmas Eve, 1928, Strom in the crow's
nest sighted it.

The barrier is like nothing else in the world. It
is so big that one can only look at it and wonder.
Where we first saw it, it was about 150 feet high,
and stretched to east and west for a length of 400
miles. It also goes inland for nearly 400 miles, a
huge triangular mass of level-topped floating ice.

It was on the eastern end of this that we were to
live. It did not look hospitable.

Huge glaciers flow down through the Queen
Maud mountains to the south and feed the barrier,
and ice sliding down from the high land to the east
runs into it. It moves slowly outward, and from it
great icebergs break off. The Antarctic bergs are
not like those in the north. They are nearly flat and
sometimes forty miles long.

After a quick visit to Discovery Inlet, which has
been there for a long time and is apparently formed
by land, Byrd went on to the Bay of Whales. It was
closed by ice that extended out between the two
walls of the barrier.

Byrd and others went ashore to look for a place to
make camp, and finally found an indentation in the
barrier that led to a fairly level field of snow. He
called it the Ver-sur-Mer Inlet, and on the slope that
led up from it, the camp was built.

One of the reasons for selecting the Bay of

Whales was that Amundsen, the only other explorer who had stayed there, reported very few high winds. That would be good for flying.

And there was a good flying field next to the camp, a field of snow on which planes with skis could be used.

That was the beginning of Little America.

16

THERE were a lot of us on that small and dingy bark, but we felt rather small, for she was tied up to the edge of the bay ice, with white cliffs all around, and miles of snowy wilderness beyond.

Try to imagine landing on a large continent, and being the only men there. There were only penguins and seals and birds and whales to greet us.

The work of unloading houses and dogs and supplies up to what was to be the camp began at once, and Byrd had the men haul the material behind dogs. We discovered later that there were 1,600 feet of water under that floating camp, but we didn't know it then.

The Fairchild, a single-engined plane, was swung over the side, and after she had been assembled and tested Byrd and a few of us went up for short hops.

From the air our ship seemed a tiny thing in the midst of a white wilderness. There was no horizon, only a blending of pale sky and hazy white.

Byrd then made a flight to the east for a few hours. He discovered the Rockefeller Mountains in a part of the land that nobody had ever seen before.

During the unloading, which went on steadily with all the dogs harnessed in teams, the bay ice kept breaking off, and the ship had to change its position. Once, the bay ice broke up sufficiently to enable the members of the crew to force the ship nearly two miles nearer the base. This was a help to the dogs, for then they had only to pull the heavy loads five or six miles.

But men fell through the rotting ice, and Byrd was forced to move to the east, where a shelf of ice came down from the low barrier to make a sort of dock.

That worked well until one day the whole slope of snow and ice slowly collapsed. Nobody went overboard, but the center section of the Ford wing was nearly lost.

Then Byrd took a desperate chance, but it was the

only thing he could do. The *Bolling* had come in and cut out a section of the rotten ice, enabling Byrd to move the two ships a short distance south. He then moored the *Bolling* against the face of the barrier, where it was about the height of her bridge. The *City* was lashed to the port side of the *Bolling*.

With difficulty, the fuselage of the big Ford was swung out of the *Bolling's* hold and over to the edge of the barrier.

As the fuselage hung in the air, and the men were about to pull it farther in, the roll of the ships caused it to bump gently on the barrier's edge. This probably weakened the icy wall. But the Ford was safe.

Then it happened.

Byrd was in his cabin on the *City,* and I was down in the main cabin showing Captain Gustave Brown of the *Bolling* a story I had written about his arrival and the first barrier crash.

Suddenly the ship rolled far to port.

Brown, an agile, quick-witted man, was up the companionway steps in two bounds.

The *Bolling* had rolled away from the *City* as tons of snow and ice had dropped on her. Hawsers holding the ships to the cliff had snapped, and the ships were drifting out, nose to the barrier.

Captain Brown made a flying leap from the *City* to the *Bolling,* and scrambled up on the bridge.

There was confusion everywhere.

Henry Harrison, one of the meteorologists, clung to a line over the edge of the barrier, and coolly dangled there about halfway to the water.

Bennie Roth, a mechanic, who could not swim, had fallen from the barrier, and was floating around with a cake of ice under each arm.

Joe De Ganahl, a navigator, came paddling by on a

plank near which he had fallen, trying to get to Roth. Joe finally reached a large cake of ice, climbed on it, took off his shoes, and sat down. I have often wondered why he took off his shoes.

A boat was put overside, and so many men got into it that it was overloaded. Malcolm Hanson, chief of the radio department, jumped overboard to lighten the load.

Meanwhile, Byrd had run up on deck with only a flannel shirt and trousers over his light underwear.

"I can get Roth. He can't swim," he yelled.

He ran aft on the *City* with the intention of leaping over the rail, but he was stopped. With scarcely a pause he jumped over to the *Bolling* and went over her stern into the water.

Roth could hardly be seen in the brilliant sun shining on the ice and water astern of us, but the boat was reaching him.

Byrd was in a hopeless position. Nobody could swim long in that water; it was too cold. With great difficulty he made his way back to the stern of the *Bolling*. One of the anxious watchers went down on a line and tied a rope around him so he could be pulled up.

While all this was going on, a loop of rope had been thrown to Henry Harrison, the meteorologist, and with difficulty he was pulled up. He had been hanging in the air ten or fifteen minutes. When he was safe, he coolly got out a cigarette, lit it, and walked away.

Roth was reached by the boat, and he and Malcolm Hanson were wrapped in blankets and put to bed. So was Joe De Ganahl, the man on the plank. None of them seemed much the worse for their ducking.

But Byrd was in a bad way, because he had been wearing so little clothing. He was thoroughly chilled, and his legs were frostbitten. I rubbed him for more than half an hour with brandy, as we had no alcohol handy.

"I guess you know how thankful I am that nobody was lost," he said after a long time.

17

THE crash of the barrier forced Byrd to try unloading elsewhere. He returned to the edge of the bay ice, bad as it was.

By this time most of the heavy things had gone ashore, if one can use that word for floating ice, and there were three airplanes at the base.

The *Bolling* had sailed away as soon as she had finished unloading her cargo on the *City*. Not long after, the *City*, too, was unloaded and went north.

With mixed feelings we watched her disappear slowly in the frost smoke, a sort of fog that rises from the icy water. We were glad to cut our ties with civilization, but sorry, also, that we would hear nothing more from home for a year, except by radio.

All this time the group of buildings ashore had been rising. Dr. Laurence M. Gould, geologist and second in command of the expedition, was in charge of the work on shore. (Dr. Gould is now president of Carlton College, in Minnesota.)

Everyone in camp had respect and genuine affection for Gould. Although he was somewhat austere, he had a wonderful sense of humor, and could swear better than any man I ever knew, without using a single cuss word. "By the beard of the prophet" might be merely the beginning of a tirade that made men jump in mock fear.

Under his leadership the camp was slowly shaping up. Three large steel radio towers had been erected. One house that was destined to be the mess hall was up. Another house was being placed some distance away, so that if there was a break in the barrier we wouldn't all fall in.

A tunnel was dug between the buildings to save us the discomfort of going outside in a blizzard. The sides of the tunnel were lined with food boxes. The top was covered with canvas, which was quickly hidden by the snow.

In the daylight hours of that fall, the long tunnel was made beautiful by the deep blue of the ice shin-

ing at its bottom. When winter darkness came we
crept through it by feeling its walls or by using flash-
lights.

Putting the houses together was hard work.
Holes were dug in the snow so that the buildings
would be buried about halfway up their sides. This
was not necessary, as it turned out, for before the
winter had really begun the houses were buried by
the drifting snow. Only their stove pipes and venti-
lators showed.

Back of the mess hall, where men slept in double
bunks, the Norge House was put up. It was so
called because it had been built in Norway. Several
men slept there. Between that and the mess hall
was a machine shop, with an engine that supplied
electricity for the radio and power for Victor

Czecha, our machinist. He could make anything.

Quinn Blackburn, one of the dog drivers, built a snow house off the tunnel where he lived most of the winter. Chris Braathen and Arthur Walden, the latter an old Alaskan dog driver, had a tiny house put together from old engine crates. They heated it with a stove made from an empty gasoline drum, and used seal blubber for fuel. It was one of the pleasantest and most peaceful spots in camp.

Frank T. Davies, the physicist, called "Taffy" because he was Welsh, made a snow house off the tunnel for his instruments. Nearby, another large snow room was dug, where many of the men boxed until it got too cold.

Still another house was built for the radio supplies and the extra parts for the planes. There was also a general storehouse dug off the tunnel.

Altogether it was quite a village.

Chips Gould, our carpenter and one of the most stoical people around camp, had one of the hardest jobs during this period. It was his duty to put up the houses.

Chips had to warm the nails on a stove before he drove them. In that below-zero temperature they became so brittle that they broke if they were used cold.

Once during the winter, the dog drivers broke

the handle of an axe with which they had been cutting up frozen seal meat for the dogs.

Chips made a wonderful axe handle of a piece of pipe.

"That will last you," he said, proudly.

But, alas, Chips forgot what cold does to iron and steel. The wonderful axe handle snapped after a few strokes. Only wood would serve.

18

WHILE the village was taking form, men were also out killing seals. Dozens of these were needed to feed the dogs, and we ate some of the meat ourselves.

In a large refrigerator aboard the *City* was some meat that Byrd had brought from the States. There were even turkeys and chickens for feast days. There were also little kidneys from New Zealand, with which George Tennant, our cook, made delicious stews.

We had only two meals a day, breakfast and dinner. The meteorologists went away mysteriously about noon to take what they called an "ob." We thought they meant observation, but it was not long before we discovered that they had been getting a few things to eat from George!

After that a regular "ob" was established. It

might consist of any cold meat or leftover beans and bread with canned New Zealand butter. It was a pretty good "ob"!

Although we had a lot of eggs, we depended largely on seal or whale meat for food. A frozen egg is an odd-looking thing when it thaws out. The yolk stays round, and the white gets very thin. We used to sigh for fresh eggs. For side dishes, we had plenty of dehydrated vegetables, and canned fruits and tomatoes.

I learned to like whale meat. When it is fresh and

ground up it tastes like hamburger. When cold it may taste like roast lamb.

Seal is dark and somewhat fishy in flavor. We even ate penguin, which is darker than seal, and even fishier. We did not like it.

The seals were big, lazy animals which seemed to sleep most of the time. They were not afraid of man because they had never before seen him. When we went near them they merely looked annoyed for a moment, gurgled, and went back to sleep.

The Adelie penguins were nearer the edge of the bay ice. They used to line up on the edge of the water, where the ice was about two or three feet high. Then they would look and look, wondering if a crab-eater seal, their great enemy, was down there.

Finally they would gang up on one penguin and push him into the water. If he lived they would all go in.

They had a game that I have seen described by only one other man. They would find a little hill of snow about three feet high, and one of them would climb to the top. The other penguins would gather at the bottom in a circle and look up at him very solemnly.

He would stare off into the distance as if quite unaware of those around him, and flap his flippers a couple of times. He would almost appear to be yawning with the boredom of it all.

Then another penguin would waddle up the slope and push the first one off. The new arrival at the top of the hill would in turn look bored and flap his flippers until *he* was pushed off by a third penguin. And so they would play their little game until each one had had a turn at the top.

These little Adelie penguins are afraid of nothing on earth. I once saw one of them run through a dog team that was lying down in harness, resting. As he went by, he pecked at the big animals.

When he had passed, the dogs realized that they had been insulted. They didn't know quite what had happened, so they started a fight which the drivers had to stop with the heavy butts of their driving whips.

The Adelie lost no time in getting away from the squabble. Then, quite unconcerned, he preened himself.

There was another incident that I remember.

When the Fairchild was first put on the bay ice it made a great deal of noise as the motor started. Snow swept out behind it. Not far in back of the airplane a little Adelie popped up on the ice.

The penguin had never heard anything quite so noisy as the airplane and, as curiosity is one of its strong points, it decided to look into the matter.

It waddled toward the plane, wondering, no doubt, what sort of bird this was. Just as it got to the tail of the plane the pilot opened the throttle, and a curtain of snow swept back.

The little Adelie tumbled head over heels out of the drift and rolled over and over until it could get to its feet.

Then it let out a squawk of dismay, shook itself, waddled to the edge of the ice, and jumped in.

"This is no place for me," it seemed to say.

It was also at the edge of the bay ice that the killer whales used to appear, sticking up their heads now and then to look at us with their mean eyes. They were after seals.

One day, while the ships were still there, Commander Byrd wanted to look at the barrier to the east of us.

He took one of the quarter boats with an outboard motor. With him were Strom, John Sutton, an engineer, myself, and Paul Siple, the Boy Scout.

The first part of the trip was enjoyable. It was a dark, gray day, with little spits of snow that rattled against our cloth parkas.

Byrd went a considerable distance south, hunting for a landing place, and then turned back toward the ship. The motor, not made for such cold weather, died. Byrd and Strom struggled with the heavy oars, and managed to move the boat a short distance. It was all I could do to swing one of the oars, for they were heavy.

Siple and Sutton, who had kept cranking the engine, finally got it going, and we headed north again in comfort.

After a time we looked ahead and saw the spouts

of two or three small whales coming in our direction.

At first we hoped they were finners, which are harmless, but after a time we saw the high fins that told us they were killer whales. These whales have real teeth, like the sperm whale.

That was not so good.

Sitting in the bow with Strom, I felt uncomfortable, to say the least. So did the others. We didn't say much about it, but I know I had trouble lighting my pipe.

We knew that killers had attacked men on the ice near the edge, and we wondered what they might do to a small boat. We would probably make a very satisfactory meal.

As we approached the killers, Byrd took the tiller. We were close to the edge of the ice, watching every movement of the whales. Just before we reached them they dived under us. When they came up again they were headed in our direction.

That was enough for Byrd. He turned the nose of the boat toward the ice, and told me to get out with the painter as soon as we hit.

When the boat struck the ice I immediately jumped out and held the rope while the others scrambled out onto the ice. We separated without a word. If those killers broke the ice they weren't going to get all of us!

Byrd had a pistol and pulled it out. Strom did the same with his.

"I wonder what effect a bullet would have on a killer," Byrd said, with a grin. "Not much, I imagine."

After a few tense minutes in which nothing happened, we decided that the killers had given up the hunt. We got back into the boat, the motor was started, and we headed for the ship. As I was in the bow I was told by Byrd to keep a sharp eye out for killer whales. Never was a watch better kept!

When we got to the ship we learned that the killers had passed there a short time before.

19

THEN came an accident that might have spoiled the expedition.

Larry Gould wanted to go to the Rockefeller Mountains to examine the rocks in that unknown part of the continent.

Byrd was reluctant to let Gould go, but he could not very well refuse. Gould knew the dangers, for it was late in the season, but he was longing to do some geological work. After all, that was really why he was down there. As there were three planes he could use one.

So Gould started off one day early in March, which is fall in the Antarctic. He took the single-engined Fokker, with Balchen piloting, and Harold June acting as radio operator. There could not have been a better team.

They reached the foot of the Rockefellers, about 125 miles east of the camp, and Balchen set the plane down on snow that was not far from an ice field.

Then Gould went to work collecting rock specimens for later study. The plane was tied down, and the men lived in a tent.

They were quite comfortable until a blizzard blew up. It did not seem serious at first, but as it continued it blew so hard that the plane was lifted and jarred down again on the snow. The wings had been tied to ropes that were fastened to heavy bits of wood buried in the snow. "Dead men," they were called.

But the "dead men" were not enough. Balchen and June dug blocks of snow with their knives, and so did Larry Gould when he was not trying to hold the plane down. Then they piled the snow blocks on the skis of the plane.

Over the wings they threw ropes, and June and Gould hung on to them until Balchen had fastened the extra ropes and piled all the snow he could on the skis.

Lumps of snow and ice from the mountains not

far away pelted them. Gould later estimated that the wind had blown 150 miles an hour. (We had a storm at the same time at Little America, 125 miles away, but our storm was in the puppy class—it blew only sixty miles an hour!)

The men had done all they could. There was nothing left but to huddle in their tent, which had snow blocks piled all around it. They wondered why they were not blown away, and at times it seemed that very thing would happen.

For hours the wind shrieked and howled around the little tent. The men couldn't have seen anything but drift if they had gone out, and they certainly could not have stood up.

When the wind let up a little, they went outside.

The plane was gone.

It had ripped loose from the lines and lifted into the air. Then it had plunged down not far away, where it lay in the snow, a total wreck.

Balchen stretched himself out and wriggled his way over to it, jabbing his knife in the snow to keep from being blown away.

The fuselage and the engine were smashed, and even the radio was not working. The tips of the propeller blades were bent, as if the plane had nose-dived. So fierce had been the force of the wind that it had turned the engine over, despite the almost frozen oil. The propeller had been whirling, as if in flight.

June fixed the radio so he could hear the operator at Little America trying to reach him, but he could not answer.

After two days Byrd prepared to send out dog teams to get the three men.

"I should never have let them go," he said. "I knew I shouldn't at this time of year, but it seemed necessary. I shall never forgive myself if anything happens to them. They are my responsibility." He was an unhappy man as he sat there holding his little dog in his lap.

At last the weather became good enough for a take-off, and Byrd decided to take the Fairchild and fly to the Rockefeller Mountains. Dean Smith, an experienced bad-weather flier and one of the best of the pioneer air-mail pilots, had the controls. Malcolm Hanson went along as radio man.

It was a rough, bumpy take-off, but Smith made it without cracking the skis. Halfway to the mountains the weather ahead was so threatening that it did not seem possible to continue without disaster. But both Byrd and Smith were determined on their course. Neither would suggest turning back.

They sighted the tent, and although the weather was rough Dean set the plane and its heavy load down lightly.

Byrd has never mentioned this, and he asked me not

to do so at the time, but that was twenty years ago. When the plane had landed he took his sleeping bag off to one side and knelt down in prayer for a time.

Again he had been saved the anguish of losing men.

Eventually they were all flown back in two trips, Byrd and Hanson staying behind until the others were safely back in camp.

The visibility was so bad on the second trip that

Dean could not see the surface of the barrier. He had to head north and follow the edge of the barrier, which was outlined by darker shadows, until he could again turn south for Little America.

It was a dangerous and efficient bit of flying.

Gould used to be teased about being "lost in the mountains."

"I never was lost," he would yell back in mock rage. "I knew where I was all the time!"

20

BLIZZARDS became more frequent. There was more darkness. It was time for Byrd to get his camp ready for winter.

The main task was to get the supplies from the barrier, where they had been dumped when taken from the two ships before the break. By this time they were buried in snow.

The flags that marked them had been carelessly moved, and as all the supplies had not been placed together, the men had to dig and search for them. It was a back-breaking task.

One day the men were shoveling wearily when

136

Taffy Davies, our physicist, hit a suspicious-looking bundle. When he finally got it uncovered, he moaned, "It can't be. Why should it be me? It's snow shovels!"

Taffy was almost ready to quit in disgust. It was recalled that when Amundsen went to the South Pole he had forgotten to take along snow shovels. Now we had too many of them! Later Taffy said: "I know more about snow than any other physicist in the world. After all, I have handled more of it."

We found strange supplies out on that barrier, such as cough drops, of which we ate a few. There were quantities of popping corn, too, and all that winter we popped it in a frying pan.

After digging all day, the men used to come in worn out. My only task during this time was to act as Byrd's housekeeper. I kept the fire going, melted snow for drinking water, and tried to keep his house swept out.

About this time holes were dug in the snow for the airplanes. Those holes were undoubtedly the world's coldest hangars. Snow blocks had been put up around them as walls, and over their tops tarpaulins were stretched to make roofs. These were soon covered with snow.

Just before the planes were put away, Alton Parker, one of the pilots, came by and looked at them. The big Ford stood on the snow, with the little Fairchild beside it. With a grin, Parker said, "It looks just like a little bird come home to its mama."

The planes were slid into the holes, and the wings of the Ford were buried in the snow. If the cold did not harm them, nothing would.

At the time we had one near tragedy. After the supplies were dug out on the barrier, they had to be hauled in by dog teams.

Quinn Blackburn, who was driving a team, did not come in one night. There was a small snowstorm, and as it was possible to see only a few yards in any direction we supposed he had been lost in it.

Everybody was worried. Drivers were supposed to keep each other in sight, but Quinn was apt to go off on his own at times.

Byrd was a member of the first party to go out and look for him. They searched for three hours, and returned half blinded by snow.

More members of the expedition were organized in groups to go out in search of the missing man. They had ropes so that they could be tied together if they went near the edge of the barrier.

In the houses men played cards with little interest in the game. What might be happening outside was not mentioned. It was tough to realize that a man everybody liked might be dying out there.

During the storm the visibility was so strange that while Joe De Ganahl was searching, he thought he saw a dog running over the snow. When he reached the place he found that it was only a small piece of paper.

In this white wilderness one group finally stumbled over Quinn. He had become lost, had dug a hole in the snow, and piled oil cans and his sledge on the windward side. Then, crawling into the hole with his dogs to keep him warm, he had gone to sleep.

He was quite annoyed that men had gone out to look for him. He had been all right, he said.

We were very much relieved when he came into the house, and began to tease him, as men will when they find the danger of tragedy is over. We told him we were glad he had enough sense to dig himself in when he found he was lost.

"The dogs wouldn't go any further," he said.

21

IN THE Antarctic, winter comes on gradually because the sun, which has been going around in a low circle, dips below the southern horizon for part of the time.

The sunset lasts for hours, and as the days pass, it gradually becomes longer and longer. At last the sun disappears and a gray twilight succeeds it. Then comes darkness for months, with only a tiny suggestion of light in the north.

Once, while the sun was below the horizon, a few of us saw what apparently no one has ever seen before or since in the Antarctic.

It was a green sun.

The reason for it is really simple. As the sun sinks below the horizon it gives off different colors. That is why we have colors at sunset—red and gold and green. Sunlight is made up of colors which blend together when the sun is high in the sky.

The last light from the sun, as it sinks, is green. We actually saw a green sun shining because the rays bent down over the horizon: a phenomenon called "refraction" by the scientists. The sight was real enough to us and could have been photographed with colored film.

When darkness falls in the Antarctic, the stars are bright because the air is so free from dirt; when the moon comes up it circles around for days before it sets again.

On clear nights we were apt to have the aurora australis, which is like our northern lights. Sometimes it resembled curtains that rippled in the sky; at other times ropes that twisted upon themselves. Once I saw a brilliant aurora that was almost overhead, spinning around like a giant pinwheel.

Around the Ford in the snow hangar, space had been left so that pilots and mechanics could work. They had to replace fuel lines, overhaul the engines, and straighten out things that might crack or clog.

It was cold work handling metal out in that snow house, where the temperature was always well below zero. Some warmth was provided by a primus heater that sent up a blast of blue flame. Once in a while Balchen, who had covered his hands with grease to prevent them from sticking to metal, would go over and run his hands through the flame.

"What we need here," grumbled Benny Roth, "is a warm-blooded monkey with cold hands."

Work was going on in all the houses, too, in preparation for our two great projects. The flight to the pole had to be made, and in the spring the geological party must start out. There were a thousand things to be done before either of these could be attempted.

Commander Byrd and his pilots, Balchen, Smith, June and Parker, discussed day after day the problems that had to be met. All winter Balchen worked with his slide rule on performance figures of the Ford, until he knew exactly what the plane would do and what it would not do.

The problem was how to carry four men, with all the food and equipment they would need if forced down, and the fuel that was necessary to get them to the pole and back.

They at last decided to establish a depot of supplies and fuel at the foot of the Queen Maud Mountains, about 400 miles south. The depot would be directly on their path back from the pole.

Captain Ashley McKinley, third in command of the camp, took part in many of these discussions, for he was to be the aerial photographer, mapping the country with his cameras.

McKinley's job during the winter was an almost impossible task. He had to develop the pictures of the flights to the Rockefeller Mountains, and later develop other pictures.

Making a dark room was easy enough, but inventing a way to melt snow for 200 gallons of

water each time he developed aerial film was a problem. Just try to melt a pail full of snow some time and see how much water you get! But it was done.

In the building where the Commander lived was the library, where I wrote my stories for *The New York Times*. In the same building was the office of the meteorologists, where they kept track of the weather and recorded the balloon ascensions that went on outdoors all winter long.

Under each balloon was a little candle so the balloon could be watched in the darkness, but the weather was often so cold that the candles would not light outdoors. The only way to light them was to warm them up on the stove indoors.

Watching balloons in the Antarctic through a metal theodolite which had to be adjusted all the time was probably the coldest job of the expedition. Harrison, who did this work, used to come in at the end of his watch, grim with cold, to warm his hands over the fire. But he never said a word. If ever I saw a stoical man it was Harrison.

Taffy Davies' hole in the snow, where the physicists' instruments were kept, was no hothouse either. He used to sit there on a box looking through his instruments for hours at a time.

One day he put his boots on the stove to dry them out. Larry Gould looked at them and shook his head sadly.

"Taffy, being a physicist, doesn't know that leather burns," he said. "So he puts his boots on the stove."

The cold did strange things when it got to 60 below zero or lower. Insulation on wires snapped. Sponge rubber would crumble in the hand. Mercury dropped on the snow would solidify instantly like hot lead on a stone. Flashlight dry batteries would freeze and die, and the kerosene in my lantern would turn to slush and the lantern would go out.

But the strangest thing was to hear one's breath freeze while facing a mild wind. The little crackles made by the freezing of moisture could be heard as they went past the ears, and were like the swish of sea water running back over the sand as a wave recedes. They were faint, but unmistakable.

Dean Smith doubted that it could happen, but one day after he was persuaded to listen, he let out a yell:

"I hear it! I hear it!"

When it was very cold there was also a mild crackling sound on the snow, and if one looked closely countless little cracks could be seen on the surface, caused by contraction.

In the crevasses around the camp were beautiful ice crystals, some as large as dinner plates, others as small as little mushrooms.

The winter was not an easy time. Men sometimes got on one another's nerves. But on the whole we were a fairly contented group, particularly when there was work to be done. We found that men whom we had not thought much of developed kindness and consideration for others. One of the loudest and most vulgar men in camp had a kind heart which manifested itself in many ways. As Dana Coman, the doctor, said:

"I have found that the longer you know a man the better you like him."

This tolerance and understanding and good nature, the constant work, and the fact that Americans are notably scoffers made our winter pass fairly peacefully.

22

A GOOD part of the work during the winter had
been directed toward getting Commander Byrd and
his men away on the polar flight. It was November,
1929, before that could be done.

November marks the beginning of the Antarctic
spring.

During the winter Balchen and Strom had made
some Norwegian sledges from skis and uprights
which they whittled with knives and then lashed
together with rawhide.

Flexible and strong, they were among the most
beautiful sledges that had ever been used for polar

147

work, and were added to the other sledges which Dr. Gould was to take on his geological trip south. It was to be a long haul, more than 1,500 miles, mostly on foot.

Meanwhile, a snowmobile party, consisting of George Black and Jim Feury, had gone south to relay supplies. Strom was sent along to take care of them, for neither had ever been alone on the ice. Byrd never had much faith in the snowmobile, which was nothing but a Ford car on skis. Nevertheless, Black, the pugnacious little supply officer, and Feury, a good-natured, lanky fellow, had been sure they could go to the pole with it.

Early in November Dr. Gould and his party started out. They had been gone only a day when they met the snowmobile party walking home!

It developed that about seventy-five miles south the snowmobile had broken down, and the three men had had to start walking back, pulling a sled. Strom, on skis, did most of the pulling, for he was a powerful man. And he knew how to tell north from south by means of his watch. This is a neat trick, but it can be done.

The snowmobile party was received with rockets, a make-believe movie camera, and strips of paper thrown from the radio towers.

Gould and his men drove on south, over dangerous crevasses and into the heart of Antarctica.

During this period of good weather, the mechanics and pilots had been at work on the Ford. The big plane, which Byrd named the *Floyd Bennett,* had been hauled out of the snow hangars with its smaller companion.

The wings, which had been buried, were dried out with blow torches, and fastened on. The engines were tuned up. Parker took it up on its first flight, and I went along. We all wondered if the wings would stay on after all this time.

They did.

The base out near the mountains was established, the plane flying over the geological party. The Ford ran out of fuel on the way home, and Smith landed her in some rough snow. But after some difficulty she was refueled and brought in.

The weather was now the deciding factor in the polar flight. And it had been found by Bill (Cyclone) Haines, our chief meteorologist, that a steady wind from the south brought dry cool air and fair skies. The drawback was that it was a headwind. which used up gas. That made a refueling depot necessary.

Thanksgiving Day, November 25, 1929, brought with it exactly the kind of weather Commander Byrd had been waiting for. There was a mild breeze from the south and only a slight haze which, Haines said, would disappear as the plane went south.

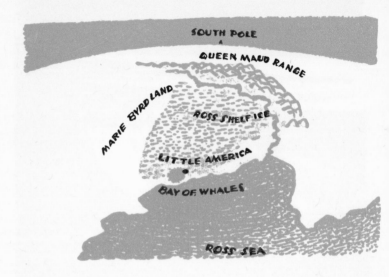

The geological party radioed in that the weather near the mountains was perfect. Haines told Byrd that he could hardly hope to get a better day.

So the plane was loaded, everything being weighed to make sure the total weight was not more than 15,000 pounds, which was the limit. There were sleeping bags, fuel, food, a sled, stoves, and McKinley's cameras.

Everyone who was to go on the flight—Byrd, McKinley, June and Balchen—took baths and put on clean underwear.

Byrd flipped the tail of his parka and laughed as he entered the plane. He is a handsome man, small, wiry and strong, and he never looked better than he did at that time.

The door to the plane was slammed, and the heavy ship taxied out to the western end of the flying field. It was a terrific test for the skis, which had been designed by Balchen, but they withstood the strain.

In a few minutes the plane was in the air and vanishing in the slight haze to the south.

Most of the rest of us went back to the mess hall, where the radio was situated. After a time June, up in the plane, tied down the sending key on his radio, and we could follow the hum of the motors through the generator of the plane's set. So long as that hum lasted, we knew Byrd and the others were safe in the air.

The hum stopped once when they were going over the mountains, probably because of interference, and everyone jumped up, tense and worried. But then it started again.

Up in the plane the men watched instruments. Byrd checked his drift by looking down through the trap door, and maintained his course with the sun compass. This gave a true direction at all times and did away with the necessity of taking continuous sights.

As he passed over the geological party, Byrd dropped a small parachute, which carried down a parcel containing some things that Gould wanted.

Then Balchen opened the motors wide, and headed for the mountains, climbing as fast as he could.

Now came the real tussle.

Could the plane climb high enough to get over the passes through the mountains, which were at an altitude of between 10,000 and 11,000 feet?

Byrd wondered whether to go up the Axel Heiberg Glacier, which had been Amundsen's route to the pole, or slightly to the west and climb up over the unexplored glacier which Amundsen had named Liv's Glacier.

He finally decided to try Liv's, as the weather there looked clearer.

June was opening fuel tins and emptying them into a tank, as unmoved as though he were on the ground instead of entering a dangerous pass where all of them might be killed.

Balchen, in the pilot's seat, was nursing the engines. He was getting every bit of power out of them and every bit of climb from the plane.

And he had to proceed with care, for on each side of the pass great peaks towered. The pass was narrower at the top than at the bottom, and riven with crevasses and falls and terraces. It was a formidable-looking place.

The plane was caught in heavy down drafts and

the flying was rough. In the rarefied air the controls were sluggish.

As Balchen neared the top of the pass he saw that he could not fly high enough with the load he was carrying.

Something had to be done, and quickly.

Balchen sent word back that 200 pounds must be thrown overboard.

June had his hand on the dump valve, but they could not let gas go. It had to be food. A bag weighing 125 pounds was dragged to the trap door by McKinley and thrown out.

"More," Balchen shouted.

Another 125-pound bag of food was thrown out. The men saw it burst open on the glacier.

All their food had now been thrown overboard, and if they were forced down they would starve. But it was a chance that had to be taken.

The plane responded as if it had been alive. It jumped upward and cleared the pass by 500 feet. Balchen yelled with joy.

All this time McKinley was silently and calmly grinding out pictures.

The engines were now purring smoothly, and there was plenty of fuel to get back to the supply base at the foot of the mountains.

Only once did one of the engines sputter. A quick

test showed that the fuel mixture had been made too lean, and this fault was quickly corrected.

They flew on south over a trackless waste of snow that seemed to head downward a little toward the pole, as if it were the rim of a huge saucer. How far above it the men were flying they could not tell, but Byrd thought it was about 1,000 feet.

At this point June relieved Balchen at the controls. Then Balchen went back into the cluttered cabin to stretch and move about. The inside of that plane was a cold and cheerless place. It was all metal except for the equipment.

Byrd was checking drift through the trap door and watching his sun compass.

The fliers saw a range of huge mountains to the

east, but it was not possible to tell in which direction they ran. Directions near the pole are hard to check.

For three and a half hours they flew south. Then Byrd made two observations which checked with the sun compass and showed they were a few miles from the pole.

When they thought they were at the pole, Byrd dropped the United States flag attached to a stone from Floyd Bennett's grave.

Having achieved their goal, the flying explorers turned back. Once more the mountains came in sight, and they found the Axel Heiberg Glacier. They flew down that, and then Byrd turned east for a time to explore the area where Amundsen thought he saw land. But there was no land there.

Snow and air conditions play such tricks with sight in the polar regions that Amundsen's error was not strange nor unusual. On his way to the North Pole, Peary thought he saw Crocker Land, which did not exist.

Again Byrd and his men turned back to the supply base at the foot of the mountains, and this time they landed. June did this landing job, because he had been there before. They refueled and took off for Little America, reaching it about nine hours after they had left the pole.

The men back at Little America had been listening to the hum of the motors over the radio and to the few messages that June had sent. They rushed out onto the field when they knew the plane was approaching.

As it taxied up to the radio towers Balchen, at the controls, had a broad grin on his face.

The door of the plane opened and Byrd appeared. He was lifted on to the shoulders of cheering men. Then they picked up June and McKinley and Balchen, and took them into the mess hall.

The hard work of months had been worth-while for every one of them.

Dick Byrd, who had been the first to fly to the North Pole, had also been the first to fly to the South Pole.

And Congress made him a Rear Admiral, as it had Peary.

23

THERE was one more mystery which Byrd meant to solve: What was the eastern boundary of the Ross Sea? This body of water was not so far away as the South Pole, but nobody had ever penetrated it to its eastern limits.

Neither the brave Captain Scott nor Shackleton, one of the greatest of polar explorers, nor even Ross, had been able to force a ship into the tightly packed ice and bergs that held the key to the secret.

I had been on the *City* when twice it had attempted to find its way toward the east through the

blinding snow and bumping ice of Ross Sea. Once the rudder froze and little bergs about as big as a house bumped alongside. It just was not possible for a ship to go very far into the Ross Sea.

An airplane could do it.

A short time after his polar flight Byrd had a good day on which he could fly to the east. In a way it was a more important flight than the one to the pole, for it was over new territory.

With Parker at the controls, Byrd took off in the *Floyd Bennett* on December 5. June and McKinley went along too, McKinley for the purpose of photographing anything that might be discovered.

It was soon found why ships had not been able to get to the east. The ice there was packed almost solid. There were many ice islands, little bergs which probably had been stranded in shallow water.

The barrier ran east for a distance and then turned north. Byrd kept well out to sea, where he could see a long range of mountains back of the shore line that ran to the north. Byrd named them the Edsel Ford Mountains. Between some of them were large glaciers.

As the party was about to turn back, June thought he saw open water to the north, and a bend of the farther coast to the southeast. Byrd wasn't sure, but it has been shown by later explorations that June was right.

On this trip the eastern side of the Ross Sea had at last been outlined. It was an important geographical discovery.

While we waited for the return of the geological party, and the coming of the ships, there was work to be done. Whatever could be taken back had to be hauled to the western side of the bay.

One day an unusual group of visitors came to the open space in the bay ice west of our frozen inlet.

There were three or four small finner whales between twenty and thirty feet long. How they got so far from the edge of the bay ice we could not imagine. It was a distance of three or four miles.

The whales poked their heads up now and then to get air, and as they slid back into the water we could see their air vents close at the back of their heads. The vents closed a split second before they reached the water. From the ice alongside we could hear them pop.

The whales were so close that we could poke them with ski sticks. And after a few hours they disappeared as mysteriously as they had come.

The geological party returned on January 19, 1930, having completed 1,500 miles of sledging. This was probably the longest sledging trip ever to be made solely for geological purposes.

The members of the party had discovered Amundsen's old cairn at the foot of the Axel Heiberg Glacier. Mountains and glaciers had been surveyed, and Gould had found almost everything he wanted except the fossil of some animal.

He had also discovered coal, which was later found east of Little America. As the British had also come upon a long seam of it to the west, it is probable that the largest coal field in the world lies under the Antarctic ice.

Gould and his crew were the dirtiest human beings we had ever seen, even dirtier than we were. Their parkas and windproofs were torn. But the men were in splendid condition, able to start out again and do another 1,500 miles.

The most remarkable thing about their trip was that none of them, with the exception of Gould, had ever been in polar regions before. Freddie Crockett, Norman Vaughan, and Eddie Goodale were in Harvard when they resigned to go south. Byrd called them the Three Musketeers.

Mike Thorne, the toughest of them all, was the son of a wealthy businessman. And Jack O'Brien, who later showed marked ability in turning out boy's books, had been a surveyor. Vaughan and Crockett were among the dog drivers who went out to get Gould when he was lost on one occasion, and on their return trip they made sixty-three miles in one day. That is traveling!

Now we waited for our ship, the *City*. The *Bolling* could not get through the ice. The ice pack that year, in January and February, 1930, was unusually heavy. Whalers reported that part of the pack was thirty-six feet thick.

It was also rapidly getting colder, an early season, and it was doubtful if our little bark could get through at all.

Those were anxious days. One man had appendicitis and had to be taken out if he were to live. He could have been operated on there, but in that case a few men would have had to stay with him and spend another winter in the Antarctic.

But the *City* found a passage in the ice, as the men aboard her told us later, and she made her way through it in thirty-six hours. Then she ran into a hurricane and was driven back into the pack for safety.

When she did get through the pack she ran into

more wind, which threw seas over her that froze when they hit. Two feet of ice formed on her hull, and ten feet of ice were on her bowsprit and martingale.

Everyone aboard was chopping away at the ice, but it coated the *City* so thickly that she kept going down by the head. At last they got into the lee of the barrier, where the seas did not wash over her. It was a close call. She had come very near sinking.

Despite all difficulties, the *City* went on until she was not far from Mt. Erebus, a live volcano at the extreme western end of the barrier, about 300 miles from us. This volcano is one of the most beautiful in the world, with long slopes, and with spouts of steam and smoke coming from its top. The men on the ship were glad to see its snow- and ice-covered sides in the distance.

As they coasted along under the lee of the barrier they chopped ice from the ship. This took them several days.

None of us who were there will ever forget the sight of the *City* coming into the camp established on the west side of the bay. The sea was covered with frost smoke, and through this we saw the ship's masts long before her hull appeared. She looked like a ghost ship.

But she was our first touch with civilization for a year. Byrd and his men were going home.

Byrd has led other expeditions to the Antarctic, and has discovered land to the east and west. But because of its spectacular achievements and the flight to the pole, his first trip there was the most interesting.

24

WHEN men go on polar expeditions they must travel either on foot or by air. They bring back outlines of the new country they have seen, or they make observations that are useful to science.

Peary and Byrd did both.

But Byrd's trip to the South Pole did much more for science than Peary's journey to the North Pole. Some of Byrd's men went hundreds of miles on foot to examine rocks; some stayed at the base and did other scientific work.

Most of Peary's work was geographical. He went

166

up the west coast of Greenland and around its northern end. He made the discovery—probably his most important work—that Greenland is an island.

Then he went across the top of Grant Land to outline the coast. He made sledge journeys to the west through Ellsmere Island, finding new bays and capes and glaciers, and doing survey work.

When he went to the North Pole he had to observe ocean currents and temperatures, but he really went to the pole only because he was determined to get there.

Byrd's work was more complicated, for by the time he went exploring the world's interest in scientific information relating to the polar regions had grown.

Men had been to the South Pole before. They had gone on foot, and they had brought back many rock samples that showed what the mountains of the Antarctic were made of. They had found coal and other metals. They had studied the bird and seal life and the ways of the penguins.

Byrd was able to see more than those who had traveled to the South Pole on foot. Flying above the earth, he had a greater range of vision. He saw many new mountains and a long range to the east. He discovered some lands on his flights to the east that men had never known or been able to reach before. He outlined a long coast.

He could not fly without meteorological observations, which meant keeping track of the weather
every hour of the day, all year long. With this information men could learn how the weather be-
haved near the pole.

They found that it was safe to fly when there are
masses of cold air coming out of the south that are
high enough to clear the sky of clouds and mist.

Byrd used meteorological observations to deter-
mine the times of his flights, for there were not
many good flying days. Today, with more information and with the instruments now carried on
planes, men can fly at either pole at almost any time.
They do so in the north even in the dark of the polar
night.

But these flights were made possible by the early
work of Byrd and others and by men who have
invented instruments to guide our planes. Byrd did
not have many instruments. He invented the first
crude bubble sextant to take sights of the sun, a
sextant which has since been greatly improved.

Air navigation has gone a long way since then,
but Byrd is responsible for some of the advances.

The meteorologists, the men who studied the
weather, also kept track of the aurora australis,
the beautiful colored lights that sometimes appear
in the sky to the south when it is dark. They also recorded all the other things that occur in the air

down there, such as the ice crystals that form and cause beautiful effects. The different layers of air that may be of varied temperatures cause strange effects, too, so that something a long way off may appear to have been lifted in the air. "Looming," it is called. A cliff miles away may appear to be hundreds of feet higher than it actually is.

Sometimes the sight of the sun or the moon is affected by ice crystals in the air. It is not unusual to see false suns around the real sun. Above and on either side of the real sun there will be golden false suns. All three are connected by a golden ring of light. And from the sun falls a pillar of golden light that ripples over the surface of the snow.

All except the real sun are illusions. But the others are real to those who watch them, as real as the sun itself.

The same thing happens to the moon; and if there is some aurora showing it can be one of the most beautiful sights in the world. They are so wonderful to see that the men of the expedition used to stand and watch them for a long time.

Once in the middle of the winter, in June—for that is midwinter at the South Pole—the meteorologists found that it was actually raining. They could hardly believe their senses, for it was only a few degrees above zero, and at one time during the day it was one degree below zero. But what they saw and felt was actually rain, water that had not turned to snow, but which froze when it touched anything. I remember my cloth parka being spotted by these frozen drops.

Larry Gould, who went out with his theodolite in the winter while there was still light, used to come in with frost all over his beard. Frost crystals covered everything at times, so that wires and anything else left outdoors had lovely crystals on them inches in length.

After working outside, Larry used to dash for the door looking like Santa Claus and yelling:

"Get out of my way! I was never so cold in my life!"

The geological party traveled 1,500 miles on foot to find many glaciers that had never been seen before, including one of the largest in the world. They found new mountains, made a map of them, and ascertained their heights.

The members of the geological party even found lichens within 300 miles of the pole. Lichens, which are among the lowest forms of life, grow on rocks.

The party's discovery of some poor coal near the tops of the mountains proved that the climate there had once been warm enough for coal formation. They also found traces of copper and other metals. Although copper is badly needed now, the Antarctic variety is poor; but even if it were plentiful it is beyond our reach.

A good deal of work was done at the base on biology; seals, penguins, and other birds were studied. Paul Siple, who was selected as the Boy Scout to go on the expedition, did much of the work. Siple was young only in years, and he did well among the older men.

Now he is Dr. Paul Siple, who does research for the United States Army on clothing and other materials for cold weather. His experiences at the South Pole have proved valuable to him in Alaska, where he often works with our soldiers. He went on both the Antarctic expeditions headed by Byrd. He was also part of two government expeditions during which Byrd was in charge of the scientific work.

Some of the most important work on the first expedition was done by Malcolm P. Hanson, a radio expert for the Navy. Hanson's work in communications really established short-wave radio, although many other men had a part in it.

When I was selected by *The New York Times* to go with the expedition and write the stories, short-wave radio was used only by "hams"—amateurs who worked all around the world with short waves. These waves could reach tremendous distances, but at that time the short-wave radio was looked upon as an interesting toy, and not very useful.

Two years before, in 1926, Hanson had built a short-wave set which was used by Byrd to communicate with *The Times* from Spitzbergen, where he took off for his North Pole flight.

Before I went south in 1928, some people doubted that my going there would be worth-while. Long-wave messages from Little America to New Zealand and then to *The Times* would have been very costly. Hanson, together with Fred Meinholtz, who had done a lot of work with short wave and who is in charge of *The Times* radio room, finally decided I might get back 1,000 words a week. That was sufficient to justify sending me.

I actually sent back thousands of words a day, and my total for the entire expedition was probably between 300,000 and 350,000 words. With Byrd's messages and other messages, the short wave carried to New York hundreds of thousands of words.

It worked so well that many radio engineers could not believe that all the stuff pouring into the office was actually sent from Little America; they thought it was being padded out in New York. Only when they went to the office and heard the messages from camp ticking in steadily did they realize what a success the short-wave radio really was.

Certainly it was invaluable for the Byrd expedition. The airplanes were equipped with it, and every sledging party had a receiver and transmitter. The result was that Byrd could keep in constant touch with every party in the field. The great tragedy of the Scott expedition might have been prevented if short wave had been available at that time.

There were two incidents I remember particularly. Once Byrd was flying out over the barrier on a short trip, and a message came in for him. It had been sent from London by cable to his New York office. From there it was telephoned to *The Times*, and directed by short wave to Little America. It was relayed to the airplane. Byrd read it, wrote an answer, and sent it back to the base. It was relayed to New York, and thence to London.

At another time Meinholtz, back in New York, left his telephone receiver off. *The Times* tried to get him on the telephone and failed. However, the operator in New York knew that Meinholtz was in the habit of listening to radio messages from us. So the New York operator asked Little America, 9,000 miles away, to tell Meinholtz to hang up his phone. He did so and his office was able to call him!

Hanson made what were probably the first polar measurements in the ionosphere. That is an electrical layer around the earth about a hundred miles up, a sort of radio roof. It is important because radio signals bounce off the ionosphere, and are able to go long distances. Men are still studying and puzzling over the ionosphere, and Hanson probed into it as well as he could with a radio he had rigged up. He even traveled miles in midwinter, when it was sixty-eight below zero, to test it.

The ionosphere reminds us that the earth is a big magnet, and that electrical currents move around it. They shift so that they make a changing pattern.

It was the work of Frank T. Davies, our physicist, to measure these magnetic currents and shifts. He had to work in a snow house that was very cold, so as to be away from everything that might interfere with his instruments. Although he wrapped himself in furs he was half frozen every evening after he got through with his job and came into the house. But he did a lot of good work, the results of which are still being used.

All these things were done in the name of exploration, for modern exploration in the polar regions has much in it beside the mere fact of going to a place where no one has been before. When a man studies geology at the poles, or makes studies useful for radio, or learns about the weather or the magnetic currents of the earth, he is exploring. His work is every bit as important as that of the man who makes his way on foot or by air to new places.

On Byrd's second trip to the Antarctic these things were done on a larger scale. When Byrd went south again in 1934 he made some dangerous flights from a ship to the coast east of Little America. They were partly in foggy weather, and once he almost lost his life by ramming an iceberg. The pilot, Harold June, just pulled up in time.

When Byrd went with other government expeditions to the Antarctic as technical adviser in charge of scientific work, the fliers who worked under him discovered much more of the coast line to the east.

Others went to the west and found one of the things which is still a mystery. They found a lake of ice-free water in a break of the mountains behind the coast. Lakes have been found in northern Greenland and other places far to the north in the summer, but this was the first time a pool of open water had been found in the Antarctic.

Whether that pool is formed by snow melting and running from the rocks, or whether it is caused by internal heat—for the Antarctic does have a live volcano or two, and may have other heat belts—is not yet known.

But there it is, one of the great mysteries of this frozen land.

The most important work of the government expeditions, aside from the flying that was done, was the testing of men and materials in cold weather.

These government expeditions consisted of many ships; the Navy even tried to take a submarine through the ice pack, but this was too dangerous and the submarine was sent back. The ships could not remain long in the Antarctic, and so the expeditions stayed only a short time.

But men learned how to protect themselves and how to test various kinds of clothing. They set up a tent city, which is probably still there. They also learned what could be done with various vehicles and other equipment.

The ships and the men were tried far beyond anything they could meet in warmer seas. Getting around in the polar regions may be very important some day.

The United States has never officially claimed a part of the Antarctic. But there may come a time when we will want to ask for our share of the continent. Then the claims of Byrd and his men must be recognized.

It is not a place where men can or will want to live for long periods. It is a place for exploration of every kind, and this country has a share in it.

And Dick Byrd led the way for us in this modern age.

INDEX